CAMPAIGN • 226

MIDWAY 1942

Turning point in the Pacific

MARK STILLE   ILLUSTRATED BY HOWARD GERRARD

Series editor Marcus Cowper

First published in Great Britain in 2010 by Osprey Publishing,
Midland House, West Way, Botley, Oxford OX2 0PH, UK
44-02 23rd St, Suite 219, Long Island City, NY 11101, USA
Email: info@ospreypublishing.com

Osprey Publishing is part of the Osprey Group.

A CIP catalog record for this book is available from the British Library.

ISBN: 978 1 84603 501 2

Ebook ISBN: 978 1 84908 295 2

Editorial by Ilios Publishing Ltd, Oxford, UK (www.iliospublishing.com)
Page layout by The Black Spot
Index by Mike Parkin
Typeset in Myriad Pro and Sabon
Maps by Bounford.com
3D bird's-eye views by Ian Palmer
Battlescene illustrations by Howard Gerrard
Originated by PDQ Media
Printed in China through World Print Ltd.

12 13 14 15 16   12 11 10 9 8 7 6 5 4 3

ACKNOWLEDGEMENTS

The author is indebted to John Lundstrom who graciously reviewed the text and clarified many points for the author. The author would also like to thank the staffs of the Naval History and Heritage Command Photographic Section (formerly the US Naval Historical Center) and the Yamato Museum and to Tohru Kizu, editor of *Ships of the World Magazine* for their assistance in procuring the photographs used in this book.

DEDICATION

The book is dedicated to my mother Louise Wilson (1930–2010).

ARTIST'S NOTE

Readers may care to note that the original paintings from which the colour plates in this book were prepared are available for private sale. The Publishers retain all reproduction copyright whatsoever. All enquiries should be addressed to:

Howard Gerrard, 11 Oaks Road, Tenterden, Kent, TN30 6RD, UK

The Publishers regret that they can enter into no correspondence upon this matter.

THE WOODLAND TRUST

Osprey Publishing are supporting the Woodland Trust, the UK's leading woodland conservation charity, by funding the dedication of trees.

Conversion table

1 inch	2.54cm
1 foot	0.30m
1 yard	0.91m
1 mile	1.61km
1 pound	0.45kg
1 ounce	28.35g

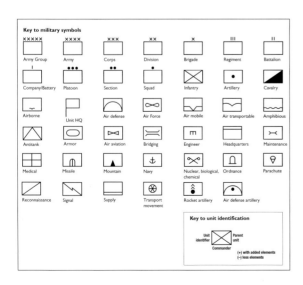

CONTENTS

ORIGINS OF THE CAMPAIGN   5

CHRONOLOGY   9

OPPOSING COMMANDERS   12
The IJN . The US Navy

OPPOSING FLEETS   16
The IJN carrier force . The US Navy carrier force . Orders of battle

OPPOSING PLANS   33
The Japanese plan: Yamamoto gets his way . The US plan

THE BATTLE OF MIDWAY   41
Opening moves . The Japanese strike Midway . The carrier battle of June 4
Midway attacks the 1st Kido Butai . Nagumo's dilemma . Fletcher's situation
The decisive phase . The Japanese response . Hiryu retaliates
Tomonaga attacks Yorktown . The death of Hiryu . Yamamoto's dilemma
Yorktown's ordeal . Spruance's battle . The pursuit phase . The accounting

THE AFTERMATH   92

FURTHER READING   94

INDEX   95

Strategic situation June 1942

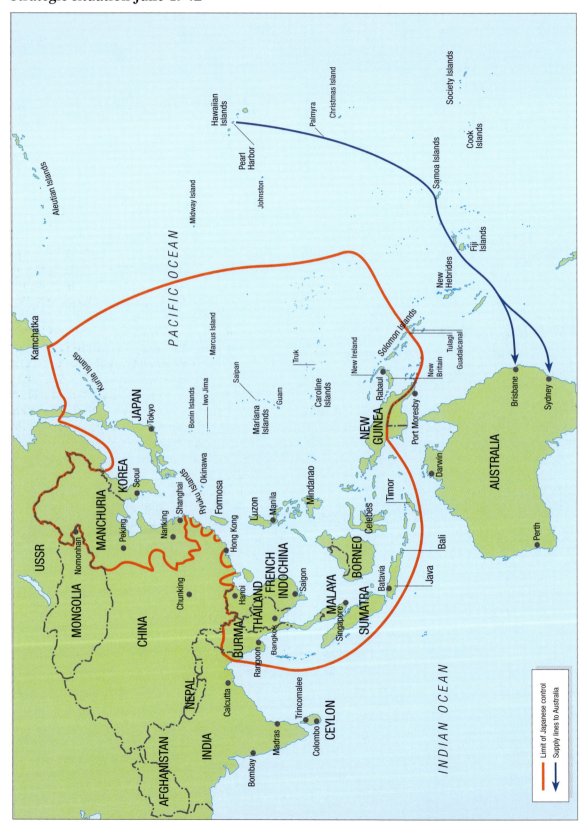

ORIGINS OF THE CAMPAIGN

Frank Jack Fletcher in the uniform of a vice admiral in September 1942. As a rear admiral, he was in overall command of American naval forces at both Coral Sea and Midway. His roles in these American victories have been largely forgotten. (US Naval Historical Center)

Few battles are as well known as the battle of Midway fought in June 1942 between the carrier forces of the Imperial Japanese Navy (IJN) and the United States Navy. The resulting victory for the Americans has been hailed as the most decisive naval battle of the entire war and an incredible victory against overwhelming odds. In fact, neither statement is true and, despite all the works about this engagement, few battles have as many myths still lingering around them as does Midway 60 years after the event.

Through April 1942, the carrier fleets of the Imperial Japanese and United States navies had yet to meet in battle. April 1942 was a key decision point for the Japanese. From the beginning of the war, they had enjoyed an unparalleled string of successes. Since assuming the defensive was unthinkable, there were basically two courses of action open to them. One, advocated by the Navy General Staff, called for the seizure of key islands in the South Pacific to cut the sea lines of communications between the United States and Australia. The other strategic option was to advance in the Central Pacific with the ultimate goal of seizing Hawaii. This was the option preferred by the Commander of the Combined Fleet, Admiral Yamamoto Isoroku, primarily because he saw the added benefit of forcing the remaining units of the US Pacific Fleet to give battle. When this decisive battle was finally fought, the superior numbers and training of the Combined Fleet would surely prevail, so Yamamoto believed.

However, what resulted from the strategic debate between the Navy General Staff and the Combined Fleet was a fatal compromise. In May, limited operations would be conducted in the South Pacific with the goal of seizing the strategic airfield at Port Moresby on New Guinea as a foundation for further expansion against Australia's sea links with the US. This would be followed in June by a massive operation against the US-held atoll of Midway in the Central Pacific some 1,300 miles from Hawaii and against selected points in the Aleutian Islands chain. Forced to defend Midway, the Pacific Fleet would be committed to action against the assembled might of the Combined Fleet.

Unfortunately for the Japanese, the American naval commander in the Pacific, Commander of the Pacific Fleet Admiral Chester Nimitz, had not read Yamamoto's script. Yamamoto was right to believe that the Americans would fight for Midway, but it was under conditions controlled by Nimitz. More than anything, Nimitz was determined to engage the Japanese aggressively as soon as favorable conditions existed. To Nimitz, favorable conditions included committing his few precious carriers even when outnumbered by the Japanese if surprise could be gained.

The four ships of the Kongo class were the only Japanese battleships with speed sufficient to provide escort to the 1st Kido Butai. *Kirishima*, shown here in 1939, was assigned to the 1st Kido Butai for the Midway operation. Behind her is *Akagi*. (Yamato Museum)

The first effect of Nimitz's policy of seeking to engage the Japanese resulted in the battle of the Coral Sea, fought between May 7 and 8, 1942. The ramifications of Coral Sea on the clash at Midway are not fully understood. The battle was the first ever contest fought between and decided by aircraft carriers. The Japanese assembled two invasion forces: one dedicated to Port Moresby and the other to the island of Tulagi in the Solomons. The invasion forces were covered by a force of heavy cruisers and a light carrier while a carrier division of two fleet carriers on loan from the Combined Fleet provided strategic cover against intervention by American carriers. After quickly seizing Tulagi on May 3, the tightly synchronized Japanese plan began to unravel. The main Japanese carrier force swung into the Coral Sea from the east to engage any American naval force there, but in spite of the fact that it had approached from a totally unexpected direction, it failed to find and destroy the two American carriers present. On May 7, both sides launched all-out strikes from their carriers. The Japanese strike totally miscarried, finding and sinking only an oiler and a destroyer. The American strike fared better, though it did not find the main Japanese carrier force. It did, however, locate and sink the light carrier covering the Port Moresby Invasion Force. On the following day, the clash of carriers finally occurred. The Japanese carriers succeeded in locating and attacking both American carriers. One was struck by a single bomb and suffered only moderate damage. However, the second was hit by both aircraft bombs and torpedoes and sank later that day. In return, a poorly coordinated American strike located only one of the Japanese carriers. They succeeded in putting three bombs into this target, but it escaped. The second Japanese carrier was untouched, but losses to Japanese carrier aircraft were very heavy.

The clash at Coral Sea had exacted a high cost from both sides. For the Japanese, the price was extremely high and constituted both strategic and tactical disaster. Strategically, the Japanese suffered their first reversal of the war. While the island of Tulagi in the Solomons was captured, the main objective of the operation, Port Moresby, remained in Allied hands. More importantly with respect to the upcoming Midway engagement, the battle had resulted in all three Japanese carriers engaged being removed from the order of battle for Midway. The light carrier *Shoho* was sunk by American carrier aircraft. The two fleet carriers that Yamamoto lent from the Combined Fleet fared better, but were both unavailable in early June. *Shokaku* was hit by three bombs and would be under repair until July 1942. Her sister ship, *Zuikaku*, was undamaged, but her air group was so battered that it would take weeks to rebuild. These losses added to the strategic disaster for the Japanese. The secondary operation at Port Moresby thus cost the Combined Fleet three of its 11 operational carriers. Most importantly, two of Yamamoto's six fleet carriers were now unavailable for Midway. As a unit, the six fleet carriers of the Kido Butai (Striking Force) was guaranteed a marked numerical advantage over any combination of operational American fleet carriers. Now this advantage was gone, and the Kido Butai would face its most severe test yet with only four of its carriers present.

American losses were highlighted by the loss of *Lexington*, while *Yorktown* suffered moderate damage. Coral Sea left only two fully operational carriers in the Pacific. These, *Enterprise* and *Hornet*, had missed the Coral Sea battle because of their involvement in the April Doolittle Raid against the Japanese home islands. Quickly dispatched by Nimitz to the Coral Sea, they arrived after the battle. The carrier *Saratoga* had been torpedoed by a Japanese submarine in January 1942 and was still under repair on the US West Coast. She was not expected back in service until late May. Thus *Yorktown*'s survival was key to the upcoming battle. Even without her, Nimitz was still determined to risk *Enterprise* and *Hornet* to take on the Japanese at Midway. However, alone they would face four Japanese fleet carriers – a daunting 1:2 inferiority. If *Yorktown* could be repaired in time, her inclusion in the battle would go far to even the odds.

Hornet at Pearl Harbor during the short respite between Coral Sea and Midway. *Hornet*'s Air Group performed dismally during the battle owing to a combination of inexperience, bad decisions, and bad luck. The ship is in a Measure 12 (modified) camouflage scheme which she would retain until her loss at the battle of Santa Cruz in October 1942. (US Naval Historical Center)

As planned by the Japanese, the operation to invade Midway and engage the remaining strength of the US Pacific Fleet would be the ultimate effort of the IJN. All eight of its operational carriers were committed, as well as the fleet's 11 battleships. Of 18 heavy cruisers, 14 were assigned roles in the operation, as were the bulk of the navy's light cruisers and destroyers. This force was under the command of 28 admirals. The IJN's largest operation of the war would consume more fuel than an entire year of normal operations. Such a force was certainly guaranteed success. Once the Pacific Fleet had been crippled, the Japanese would again turn south to cut off the sea lines of communications between the US and Australia. Hawaii itself, devoid of protection from the US Navy, was also a potential target.

For his part, Nimitz had the invaluable advantage of superior intelligence regarding his enemy's strength and intentions. This intelligence was far from omniscient, but, combined with Nimitz's innate aggressiveness and strategic insight, it guaranteed that America's remaining naval strength was placed in the best position to do the most potential damage to the Japanese. Nimitz committed all his remaining strength to defending Midway, including all three of his carriers. Pearl Harbor had not eliminated the US Navy's battleship strength in the Pacific, despite popular myth, and by June 1942 seven battleships were operational in the Pacific. Mindful of the lessons taught to him at Pearl Harbor, Nimitz resisted repeated demands that he aggressively employ his battleships and instead moved them to the West Coast out of the way. Unlike Yamamoto, Nimitz's plan for the upcoming battle was almost totally dependent upon the carriers of the Pacific Fleet. With Yamamoto throwing the entire strength of the IJN at Midway, and Nimitz prepared to defend it with his entire remaining strength, the scene was set for the single most dramatic and important battle of the Pacific War.

CHRONOLOGY

May 7 — Carrier battle in the Coral Sea. After a series of incorrect scouting reports by both sides, the Americans and Japanese launch their main carrier strike forces at secondary targets. Aircraft from carriers *Yorktown* and *Lexington* sink Japanese light carrier *Shoho*. In return, Japanese carrier dive-bombers sink a destroyer and an oiler.

May 8 — In an exchange of strikes against each other's main carrier force, the Americans score three bombs on carrier *Shokaku*, putting her out of action. The Japanese place two torpedo and two bomb hits on *Lexington*. This damage eventually proves fatal and the ship sinks later that evening. One bomb hit is scored on *Yorktown* causing moderate damage.

May 27 — The Kido Butai departs the Inland Sea.

May 28 — *Enterprise* and *Hornet* depart Pearl Harbor.

May 30 — *Yorktown* departs Pearl Harbor.

May 31 — Operation *K*, the plan to surveil Pearl Harbor with long-range flying boats refueled by submarine, is cancelled.

June 2 — US carriers rendezvous northeast of Midway.

June 3 — 0843hrs – Midway-based PBYs spot Minesweeper Group.

0925hrs – PBYs spot Transport Group.

1225hrs – Midway-based B-17s depart to attack Transport Group; no hits are scored.

June 4 — 0130hrs – PBYs conduct night torpedo attack against Transport Group hitting tanker *Akebono Maru*.

0430hrs – Nagumo launches 108-aircraft strike against Midway.

0530hrs – Japanese carriers sighted by PBYs.

0620hrs – Air battle between Midway fighters and Japanese fighter escort.

0630hrs – Midway bombed, suffering heavy damage. Antiaircraft defenses account for 25 Japanese aircraft destroyed or rendered non-operational.

0700hrs – 116 aircraft launched from *Enterprise* and *Hornet* against Japanese carriers.

0702hrs – First American air attack on Japanese carriers. Six Midway-based TBF Avengers and four B-26s score no hits.

0705hrs – Japanese strike leader against Midway informs Nagumo a second strike is needed against the island.

0715hrs – Nagumo orders his reserve aircraft armed to attack Midway.

0740hrs – Japanese scout aircraft reports American ships located north-northeast of Midway.

0745hrs – Nagumo orders re-arming process stopped.

0800hrs – 16 Marine Dauntlesses from Midway attack Japanese carriers; no hits are scored.

0820hrs – 14 B-17s attack Japanese carriers; again no hits are scored.

0825hrs – 11 Marine SB2U-3s attack battleship *Haruna*; no hits are scored.

0830hrs – Japanese search aircraft confirms presence of carrier in previously reported American task force.

0905hrs – *Yorktown* launches her strike.

0915hrs – Start of VT-8 attacks against Japanese carriers; all 15 aircraft lost for no hits.

0918hrs – Nagumo completes recovery of Midway strike; now plans a 1030hrs strike against the American carriers.

0940hrs – Start of VT-6 attack; 10 are lost for no hits.

1002hrs – *Enterprise*'s dive-bombers sight the 1st Kido Butai.

1003hrs – *Yorktown* strike spots the 1st Kido Butai.

1010–1030hrs – VT-3 and fighter escort duel with Japanese fighters; most defending fighters drawn to low level.

1022hrs – The majority of *Enterprise*'s dive-bombers attack *Kaga*; four hits are scored causing mortal damage.

1025hrs – VB-3 attacks *Soryu*; three hits are scored causing uncontrollable fires.

1026hrs – Three Dauntlesses attack *Akagi* scoring a single hit; this damage ultimately proves fatal.

1040hrs – VT-5 concludes attack on *Hiryu*; no hits are scored.

1050hrs – *Hiryu* launches strike on American carriers.

1209hrs – *Hiryu* dive-bombers commence attack on *Yorktown* scoring three hits. *Yorktown* is set afire and temporarily comes to a stop.

1331hrs – *Hiryu*'s second strike departs.

1427hrs – Strike detected by American cruiser radar.

1443hrs – Japanese torpedo aircraft put two torpedoes into *Yorktown* bringing the ship to a stop and causing a severe list.

1445hrs – *Hiryu* spotted by *Yorktown* scout.

1705hrs – *Hiryu* attacked by dive-bombers from *Enterprise* and *Yorktown*; four hits set the Japanese ship afire.

1811hrs – Fletcher passes tactical control of battle to Spruance.

1913hrs – *Soryu* sinks.

1925hrs – *Kaga* sinks.

June 5

0255hrs – Yamamoto cancels Midway operation.

0230hrs – Cruisers *Mogami* and *Mikuma* collide within 50 miles of Midway heavily damaging *Mogami*.

0520hrs – *Akagi* sinks.

0820hrs – *Hiryu* sinks.

0840hrs – Midway attacks two Japanese cruisers.

1636–1845hrs – Destroyer *Tanikaze* attacked by 43 dive-bombers and 18 B-17s; no direct hits are scored.

June 6   0945–1445hrs – Carrier dive-bombers attack cruisers; *Mikuma* later sinks, *Mogami* survives.

1336hrs – Submarine *I-168* hits *Yorktown* with two torpedoes and sinks destroyer *Hammann*.

June 7   0501hrs – *Yorktown* sinks.

OPPOSING COMMANDERS

Admiral Yamamoto Isoroku assumed command of the Combined Fleet in 1939. His daring and successful gamble at Pearl Harbor gave him tremendous influence, and when backed by the threat of resignation, ensured that he shaped Japanese naval strategy. Unfortunately for the IJN, his plans for the Midway operation provided the foundation for defeat. (US Naval Historical Center)

THE IJN

The driving figure behind the Midway battle was the commander of the Combined Fleet, **Admiral Yamamoto Isoroku**. He had a reputation for brilliance and for being a gambler. These myths were created by the Pearl Harbor operation which he personally advocated and planned. Yamamoto was fully convinced of his own brilliance and was determined to be the principal figure in shaping Japanese naval strategy. In this he was successful. In the debate leading up to the war, his threats to resign if his risky Pearl Harbor attack was not adopted swung the formulation of naval strategy into his hands. But by Midway, cracks in the Yamamoto brilliance myth were beginning to appear. It is true that the IJN had gained a string of successes against ineffective opposition, but he had yet to engage and defeat the American carriers. The April raid into the Indian Ocean by the Japanese carrier was an unnecessary strategic deadend, and the battle in the Coral Sea in May had resulted in a tactical and strategic defeat. At Midway, despite his reputation as an air-power advocate, he planned a battle more reminiscent of prewar Japanese plans for a decisive battleship clash in the Western Pacific. Despite having a massive numerical superiority and an edge in quality, Yamamoto found a way not to translate these advantages into a plan to crush the US Pacific Fleet. At Midway, Yamamoto's overconfidence laid the foundation for a crushing defeat.

The admiral charged to carry out Yamamoto's strategic design was 55-year-old **Vice Admiral Nagumo Chuichi**. He was a sea-going admiral with a background in torpedo tactics. In April 1941, he assumed command of the 1st Air Fleet. This was not because of any background in naval aviation or because his command personality was suited to carriers; rather he was the senior vice admiral needing an assignment, and the newly created 1st Air Fleet post was a vice admiral's billet, so he got the job. His command style was marked by a lack of decisiveness and reliance on his staff. Nevertheless, by June 1942, he was the most experienced carrier commander in the world.

Since Nagumo demonstrated little concern for learning the intricacies of carrier warfare, he relied heavily on his staff. His chief of staff was **Rear Admiral Kusaka Ryunosuke**. Though involved in naval aviation since 1926, he was not an aviator and did not possess a deep knowledge of air warfare. He was cautious by nature. The most important figure on Nagumo's staff was the Air Officer, **Commander Genda Minoru**. He had made his reputation as a daring fighter pilot and was the driving force behind the creation of the 1st Air Fleet. He enjoyed the complete trust of Nagumo and was given total freedom in planning operations.

The commander of Carrier Division 2, comprising half of Nagumo's carrier force, was 50-year-old **Rear Admiral Yamaguchi Tamon**. He was held in high esteem within the IJN and was even viewed as a possible successor to Yamamoto. His background was very similar to Yamamoto's – a member of the Japanese delegation at the London Naval Conference, a naval attaché in Washington, and an advocate of naval aviation. He had served with Nagumo since the start of the war and thought that his commander lacked boldness. It is certain that if the aggressive Yamaguchi had been in command of the 1st Kido Butai, the battle would have been fought differently.

The captains of the four Japanese carriers present at Midway were all experienced officers. The captain of *Akagi* was **Aoki Taijiro**. He had just taken command and this was his first combat assignment in the war. **Okada Jisaku** commanded carrier *Kaga*. He had been in command since September 1941 and had a long association with naval aviation. The only aviator of the four carrier captains at Midway was **Kaku Tomeo** of the *Hiryu*. His experience in carrier aviation dated from 1927. The skipper of carrier *Soryu* was **Yanagimoto Ryusaku**. Among his former billets were as a naval attaché, a Naval War College instructor, and head of intelligence on the Naval General Staff.

Other important command figures included **Vice Admiral Kondo Nobutake** who commanded the Midway Invasion Force. He was considered an aggressive officer and was a member of the so-called "battleship clique." Commander of the Close Support Group was **Vice Admiral Kurita Takeo**, later to command the most important Japanese force during the battle of Letye Gulf. The Transport Group was commanded by the very capable **Rear Admiral Tanaka Razio**, later to gain fame as the head conductor of the "Tokyo Express" during the Guadalcanal campaign.

Vice Admiral Nagumo Chuichi was tasked by Yamamoto with neutralizing Midway Island and destroying any intervening American naval forces. He did neither. Instead, his lack of decisiveness and a large measure of bad luck provided a recipe for disaster. (US Naval Historical Center)

THE US NAVY

More than any other American naval commander, the battle of Midway was **Admiral Chester Nimitz**'s battle. Nimitz assumed command of the US Pacific Fleet on December 31, 1941, in the aftermath of the Pearl Harbor disaster. He was the personal choice of President Roosevelt who had been impressed by Nimitz during his two tours in Washington assigned to the Bureau of Navigation (the office responsible for personnel matters). The appointment of Nimitz to assume his new command did not go down well with many other flag officers given Nimitz's relative lack of seniority and the perception that he was a political admiral. Nimitz's background, after his 1905 graduation from Annapolis, was initially in submarines and later in cruisers and battleships. He had no background in naval aviation but possessed many other qualities that would get him through the tough days to follow. Despite his background as a submariner and a surface officer, he played no favorites with the navy's competing factions. He was known as a good administrator and possessed a sense of optimism that was sorely needed in Hawaii in late 1941. He had an uncanny ability to pick good leaders and then give them the room they needed to get their jobs done. What was not clear at the time was Nimitz's aggressiveness and strategic insight. If these qualities were not apparent after Coral Sea, they certainly would be after Midway.

The most combat-experienced American carrier commander in June 1942 was **Rear Admiral Frank Jack Fletcher.** He had commanded the American carriers in the Coral Sea and was commended by Nimitz for his performance. When he returned to Pearl Harbor in the damaged *Yorktown*, Nimitz placed him in overall charge of the entire American carrier force operating off Midway. Fletcher was not an aviator, but by June 1942 had acquired a wealth of carrier experience and it was not unusual at that point in the war to have non-aviators in command of carrier task forces. Fletcher's role in the battle has been largely forgotten because of the circumstances which placed his subordinate, Rear Admiral Raymond Spruance, in charge of the carrier force for most of the time. Nevertheless, it is important to remember the important role Fletcher played executing the initial strikes which caught the Japanese carriers flat-footed.

The senior-ranking US Navy carrier commander in June 1942, and without a doubt the most aggressive, was **Vice Admiral William Halsey.** Just before the battle, and to his intense disappointment, Halsey was sidelined because of a skin disease. To replace him, he recommended **Rear Admiral Raymond Spruance.** Spruance was a surface line officer with no aviation experience. He did have some knowledge of carrier warfare, as he had been commanding Halsey's cruiser screen since the start of the war. Upon assuming command, Spruance kept Halsey's entire staff. Had Halsey been healthy, it is important to note that he, not Fletcher, would have been in command of Nimitz's carriers.

Spruance emerged from the battle with the lion's share of the credit for the victory and a reputation as a cool, calculating thinker. He was a 1907 graduate of the Naval Academy and spent his early years in destroyers. He had spent five years at the Naval War College teaching and studying, and was held in high regard as a naval strategist. In 1940, he gained flag rank and in September 1941 assumed command of Cruiser Division 5. Even he believed his lack of aviation experience would rule him out as a successor to Halsey, but on May 26, Nimitz informed him of his new command.

The captains of the American carriers at Midway were naval aviators, as were all carrier skippers as per US Navy regulation. The captain of *Yorktown* was **Elliott Buckmaster**. Buckmaster was known for his excellent seamanship and his willingness to let his aviators experiment. *Yorktown*'s Air Group was the most experienced by June 1942 and performed well during the battle. The captain of *Hornet* was **Captain Marc A. "Pete" Mitscher**. He had already been promoted to rear admiral before the start of the battle, and even though the new captain, Charles P. Mason, was on board, Mitscher would retain command during the battle. *Hornet*'s performance in the battle can be described only as dismal, but Mitscher went on to achieve great success as a carrier group commander later in the war. *Enterprise*'s skipper was **Captain George Murray**. He was a long-time aviator, being the 22nd American naval officer to be awarded his wings.

The Midway garrison was under the command of **Captain Cyril Simard**, US Navy. His command included shore-based aviation composed of Navy, Marine and Army Air Force assets, together with an island defense force built around the 6th Marine Defense Battalion.

OPPOSING FLEETS

THE IJN CARRIER FORCE

The revolutionary change in naval warfare during the initial period of the Pacific was the ability of the Japanese to mass carrier air power. This development dated from April 1941 when the Japanese assembled all their fleet carriers into a single formation, the 1st Air Fleet. The Kido Butai (literally "Mobile Force" but better known as "Striking Force") was the operational component of the 1st Air Fleet. Three carrier divisions made up the Kido Butai, each with two carriers. For the Midway operation, Carrier Divisions 1 and 2 were committed. Carrier Division 1 possessed the IJN's largest carriers, while Carrier Division 2 possessed the smaller but more nimble Soryu class. To be strictly accurate, the Midway operation included a second Kido Butai assigned to support the Aleutians attack, but the IJN's main carrier force remained the carriers under Nagumo.

The flagship of the 1st Kido Butai was *Akagi*. She was a converted battlecruiser, so possessed a high speed, good protection and a large aircraft capacity (though still smaller than the American carriers). In 1937–38, *Akagi* was rebuilt and emerged with a small island and a downward-facing stack on the starboard side, a common design feature on most subsequent Japanese carriers. After her reconstruction, *Akagi* retained six 8in. guns mounted in casemates for protection against surface attack and 12 4.7in. antiaircraft guns in dual mounts and 14 twin 25mm guns for antiaircraft protection.

Akagi, flagship of the 1st Kido Butai since its formation in April 1941. Note the three Zero fighters which have been spotted forward. (*Ships of the World Magazine*)

TOP
Kaga was the largest of the 1st Kido Butai's carriers and possessed the largest aircraft capacity. This overhead view shows her massive size, the result of her conversion from a battleship. (*Ships of the World Magazine*)

BOTTOM
Soryu, seen here in 1938, was the first Japanese fleet carrier designed as such from the keel up. Her fine lines indicate a high speed, but also a lack of protection. This reflected the IJN's carrier design philosophy that stressed offensive capabilities. (Yamato Museum)

Rounding out Carrier Division 1 was *Kaga*. Converted from a battleship, she possessed the lowest speed and was the least maneuverable of the Kido Butai's carriers, but could embark the most aircraft. Her modernization from 1934–35 gave her a configuration similar to *Akagi*'s. *Kaga*'s armament in 1942 included ten 8in. guns mounted in casemates for protection against surface attack; antiaircraft protection surpassed that of *Akagi* and included eight Type 89 dual mounts and a total of 30 25mm guns in twin mounts.

The two ships of the Soryu class epitomized Japanese carrier design philosophy with their combination of a relatively large aircraft capacity on a fast, light hull. *Soryu* was actually the first IJN fleet carrier designed from the keel up. Both carried an operational air group equivalent to the much larger *Akagi* and *Kaga*. Powerful machinery and a cruiser-type hull, combined with a high beam to waterline ratio, gave a very high speed, but protection over machinery and magazine spaces was entirely inadequate. With an extra 1,400 tons in displacement, *Hiryu* was actually built to an improved design. Additional armor was fitted in an attempt to rectify the principal design defects on *Soryu*, but it was still inadequate against attack by aircraft bombs. Both ships carried similar weapons fits of six Type 89 dual 5in. mounts and a mix of 25mm mounts. *Soryu* carried 14 double mounts while *Hiryu* carried a mix of seven triple mounts and five twin mounts.

The third carrier division of the Kido Butai was composed of the two ships of the Shokaku class. However, the Coral Sea operation had treated Carrier Division 5 roughly. *Shokaku* suffered three bomb hits and was under repair. *Zuikaku* was untouched, but her air group had taken such a beating that she was also out of action. Unlike in the US Navy, the air groups of Japanese

carriers were an integrated part of the ship's company and thus could not be easily swapped with other ships. Nevertheless, the failure to include *Zuikaku* in the Midway operation was another sign of Japanese overconfidence. After the Coral Sea operation, *Zuikaku* returned with 39 operational aircraft (24 fighters, nine carrier bombers and six carrier attack planes). On top of this, another 17 aircraft were on board and were believed to be repairable (one fighter, eight carrier bombers, and eight carrier attack planes). Thus, if the Japanese had thought it important enough, *Zuikaku* could have sailed with a makeshift air group of 56 aircraft, comparable in strength to the other carriers in Nagumo's force. The Japanese failure even to consider this option compares poorly with the energetic American efforts to get *Yorktown* to sea following her damage at Coral Sea.

IJN carrier air groups

The salient strength of the Kido Butai was its ability to conduct coordinated, large-scale air operations. As a matter of course, during 1942 the Japanese were able to handle their carrier aircraft in a manner far superior to that of the Americans. For example, at Midway, when the Japanese prepared to strike the island, 108 aircraft were employed from four carriers. The first aircraft was launched off *Akagi* at 0426hrs on June 4, and by 0445hrs the entire group headed off in a single formation for Midway. By comparison, later that same morning, it took the Americans an hour to launch 117 aircraft from two carriers. Even this did not go smoothly; when they departed the carriers, they did so in four separate groups, and, not surprisingly, were thus unable to deliver a coordinated attack.

To achieve this impressive feat, the Japanese mixed carrier divisions to assemble a combined strike of fighters, dive-bombers, and torpedo planes. One carrier division would launch its dive-bombers while the other launched its torpedo bombers. With the fighter escort of six to nine aircraft per ship, this could be achieved in a single deckload. In turn, this reduced launch times and minimized coordination problems. The balance of each carrier's strike aircraft would be launched in a second wave or held in reserve.

Combined with the superior aircraft handling doctrine, the Kido Butai possessed excellently trained and experienced aircrews. Of the carrier bomber crews, 70 percent were veterans of Pearl Harbor. The figure for carrier attack plane crews was an even higher 85 percent. Even the replacements were probably highly experienced aviators. However, after over six months of continual operations, some of the basic skills of the Kido Butai's aircrews had atrophied, as was confirmed during a short period of refresher training conducted before the Midway operation began. However, on balance, there is no question that the Kido Butai's aircrew were the best trained and experienced in the Pacific.

Finding aircraft for the Kido Butai proved to be a problem, however. Losses in the first few months of the war had been relatively light, but the aircraft strengths for the Kido Butai's carriers continued to decline. The Japanese aviation industry was unable to keep pace even with these losses, in large measure because it was transitioning to new types of carrier aircraft, and production of existing types had been curtailed. As a result, the four carriers at Midway carried 16 percent fewer aircraft than they did at Pearl Harbor only a few months earlier (if the missing ships of Carrier Division 5 were included in the calculation, then the Kido Butai carried only 60 percent of the aircraft it did at Pearl Harbor). Partly compensating for the aircraft shortage were the 21 A6M Zero fighters from the 6th Air Group intended for the Midway garrison once the island was captured. These were fully assembled and some of the pilots were carrier qualified. The situation was similar for the other four smaller carriers assigned to the Midway operation – none was carrying its full capacity of aircraft.

Each of the Kido Butai's four carriers embarked an air group with three squadrons. The air groups retained the names of their parent ship and were permanently assigned to the ship. Each of the component squadrons also retained the name of its parent carrier. Whether fighter, dive-bomber or torpedo bomber squadron, the typical squadron strength was 18 aircraft, broken down into two nine-aircraft divisions. The only exception was the Carrier Attack Unit aboard *Kaga* which had an extra division, for a total of 27 aircraft. *Soryu* embarked two D4Y1 carrier bombers (the planned replacement for the current D3A1 carrier bomber) to be used in a reconnaissance role, so *Soryu*'s Carrier Bomber Unit was reduced to 16 aircraft. The 21 A6M fighters of the 6th Air Group were in addition to the 18-aircraft fighter units aboard each of the four carriers.

Light carrier *Zuiho* pictured in December 1940. This useful carrier was assigned to the Midway Invasion Force and played no role in the battle. (Yamato Museum)

IJN carrier air defense

As proficient as the IJN was at massing and coordinating offensive air power, it also possessed an inability to defend its carriers properly. The defensive capabilities of the Japanese carriers were fatally compromised by a lack of radar and generally ineffective antiaircraft defenses. Though their damage-control capabilities had hardly been tested up until June 1942, the weakness of the Japanese carrier crews dealing with serious damage would be fully revealed at Midway.

The principal weakness of Japanese carrier air defense stemmed from a lack of early warning. Unlike American carriers, Japanese carriers at Midway possessed no radar. Thus, the only warning of approaching enemy aircraft was usually provided by lookouts. If approaching aircraft were spotted by an escort, the procedure was to lay smoke or to fire its main battery at the enemy to gain the attention of the overhead combat air patrol (CAP). Reliance on lookouts was a recipe for potential disaster, as was demonstrated in the Indian Ocean in April when nine RAF Blenheim bombers approached and bombed *Akagi* undetected, scoring no hits. At Midway, this potential for disaster was confirmed when the Japanese were constantly surprised by the appearance of American dive-bombers.

Fighter direction was an insurmountable problem for the Japanese in June 1942. Usually, half of the 18-aircraft fighter squadron was dedicated to CAP. With no radar, standing CAP was maintained over the parent carrier usually with a group of three fighters. The remaining aircraft were placed on stand-by to be scrambled once warning was received. Adding further difficulty to the problem of controlling aircraft was the inferior quality of Japanese aircraft radios that made it virtually impossible to control aircraft already airborne. The result was that there was no overall control of the Kido Butai's CAP. Allocation of aircraft to incoming threats was performed by the pilots themselves, which meant that it was impossible to coordinate a defense properly against a multi-axis, multi-altitude threat. At Midway, this easily saturated air-defense system would lead to fatal consequences.

A Zero fighter spotted aboard *Akagi*. The Zero was a formidable fighter, but its effectiveness as a fleet air defense asset was compromised by a lack of adequate early warning and an effective system of airborne control. These weaknesses would be fully exposed at Midway. (*Ships of the World Magazine*)

If attacking American aircraft broke through the CAP, they still had to contend with the antiaircraft defenses aboard every Japanese carrier. However, while in theory Japanese carriers were equipped to conduct long-range antiaircraft fire with their 5in. guns and short-range fire with their 25mm guns, neither layer of protection proved effective in practice. In fact, *Akagi* did not even have the newer 5in. guns, but still retained the older 4.7in. weapon with a slower rate of fire and inferior elevation. *Kaga* did have the new 5in./40 Type 89 dual mount, but was equipped with a dated fire-control system. *Soryu* and *Hiryu* were equipped with the new Type 89 and the latest Type 94 fire-control system, but the Type 94 was unable to track and engage fast targets (like a dive-bomber in a dive). The Type 96 25mm gun served as the last-ditch defensive weapon, but was ineffective in this role. Even the Japanese recognized that it could not handle high-speed targets because it could not be trained or elevated fast enough by either hand or power and its sights were inadequate for high-speed targets. It also demonstrated excessive vibration and muzzle blast, and its magazines were too small to maintain high rates of fire. Even when the Type 96 managed to hit its target, its small weight of shell (.6 pounds) was often ineffective against the rugged American aircraft. The general ineffectiveness of Japanese antiaircraft capabilities is dramatically shown by the fact that of the 144 American aircraft lost during the battle, only about five were destroyed by antiaircraft fire.

Given the weakness of Japanese shipboard antiaircraft gunnery, the most effective form of defense from air attack was skillful maneuvering. Radical maneuvering was the norm for a ship under attack, though this made it even more difficult for any escort to provide support and for the maneuvering ship to generate correct fire-control solutions for accurate antiaircraft fire. The threat of American torpedoes could easily be defeated by appropriate maneuvers since the Mark 13 US Navy torpedo had a top speed of only 33 knots and could simply be outrun. However, against a well-trained dive-bomber pilot, maneuver did not provide the same degree of immunity.

IJN carrier aircraft

Japanese carrier aircraft in June 1942 were clearly superior to their American counterparts in two areas – fighters and torpedo bombers. The Japanese dive-bomber was also a very capable design, but was not the equal of the American Dauntless. The Japanese used a design philosophy that stressed maneuverability and range. To achieve this, Japanese carrier aircraft were much less protected and lacked the ruggedness of similar American aircraft.

The standard IJN carrier fighter was the A6M Type 0 (later given the codename "Zeke" by the Allies but called "Zero" by both sides). The Zero had met the standard American carrier fighter for the first time at Coral Sea and its superiority was acknowledged even by the Americans. It possessed exceptional maneuverability, great climb and acceleration, and a powerful armament. However, lacking armored protection and self-sealing fuel tanks, the Zero was vulnerable to damage.

The Japanese called their dive-bombers "carrier bombers." The standard carrier bomber in June 1942 remained the D3A1 Type 99 Carrier Bomber (later codenamed "Val" by the Allies). The D3A1 was well designed for conducting precision dive-bombing attacks and had proven to be a deadly weapon in the hands of an experienced pilot. Though built to withstand dives of up to 80 degrees, it did not carry self-sealing fuel tanks and could not carry as heavy a payload as the American Dauntless.

A Type 97 Carrier Attack Aircraft landing aboard the carrier *Shokaku*. This aircraft, combined with its reliable air-launched torpedo, gave the air groups of Japanese carriers a deadly ship-killing weapon. They could also carry a large bomb load, as they did to attack Midway on the morning of June 4. (Yamato Museum)

The real striking power of Japanese air groups against large ships was provided by what the IJN called "carrier attack planes." These were primarily designed to act as torpedo bombers, but also carried bombs for use against land targets. In June 1942, the standard carrier attack plane was the B5N2 Type 97 (later codenamed "Kate" by the Allies). What made the B5N2 so effective was its primary weapon, the Type 91 Mod 3 Air Torpedo. This 17.7in. diameter weapon contained a 529-pound warhead and was capable of traveling at 42 knots for up to 2,000 yards. The combination of the B5N2 and its reliable and effective torpedo gave Japanese air groups an effective ship-killing power not possessed by American carriers of the day. However, the B5N2 exchanged its range and performance for a lack of protection.

THE US NAVY CARRIER FORCE

The US Navy began the war with seven fleet carriers. Of these, the *Ranger* and *Wasp* were in the Atlantic in June 1942. This left the five ships of the Lexington and Yorktown classes to oppose the advancing IJN. Fortunately, none of the Pacific Fleet's carriers were present in Pearl Harbor on the day of the attack, but shortly thereafter on January 11, 1942, Lexington-class carrier *Saratoga* was torpedoed near Pearl Harbor by a Japanese submarine. The damage was severe enough to make *Saratoga* miss both Coral Sea and Midway. *Lexington* was one of the two carriers committed by Nimitz to oppose the Japanese advance into the Coral Sea in May 1942. In this first carrier clash with the Japanese, *Lexington* took two torpedo and three bomb hits from Japanese carrier aircraft. Though initially it looked like she would survive this pounding, leaking gas vapors as a result of the battle damage caused massive explosions resulting in the loss of the ship on May 8, 1942. In the same battle, *Yorktown* was moderately damaged by a single bomb hit and a number of near misses, but survived. Thus as Nimitz was planning his response to the expected Japanese advance into the Central Pacific, he had only the three carriers of the Yorktown class to oppose the Japanese.

TOP

Enterprise docked at Ford Island, Pearl Harbor. The ship's CXAM-1 radar is evident on the foremast. Battleship *California* is under salvage to the left. (US Naval Historical Center)

BOTTOM

Yorktown in dry dock at Pearl Harbor undergoing urgent repairs for damage received during the battle of Coral Sea. The efforts of the Americans to return *Yorktown* to service contrast dramatically with the Japanese attitude to preparing carrier *Zuikaku* for action following her participation in Coral Sea. (US Naval Historical Center)

The Yorktown class was designed with the benefit of fleet experience and proved to be very successful in service. These 20,000-ton ships were large enough to permit the incorporation of protection against torpedo attack. A 4in. side armor belt was fitted over the machinery spaces, magazines and gasoline storage tanks. Vertical protection was limited to 1.5in. of armor over the machinery spaces. At Midway, *Yorktown* took a beating from torpedoes and bombs in excess of the expectations of her designers before finally succumbing. The primary design focus of the class was to provide adequate facilities to operate a large air group quickly and efficiently. This design emphasis and the fact that American carriers routinely operated a deck park of aircraft meant that they embarked more aircraft than their Japanese counterparts.

The Yorktown class also received a heavy defensive armament to counter Japanese air attack. This class was among the first US Navy ships equipped with the new 5in./38 dual-purpose guns that proved to be the best long-range antiaircraft weapon of the war. Four 1.1in. quadruple mounts were placed fore and aft of the island and 24 .50-cal. machine guns were originally fitted for close-in protection. By June 1942, the ineffective machine guns were being replaced by 20mm automatic cannons. *Hornet* and *Yorktown* each received 24 20mm guns and *Enterprise* received 32. All three ships carried radar. *Yorktown* received one of the first six CXAM sets in October 1940 and *Enterprise* received the improved CXAM-1. *Hornet* was initially fitted with the disappointing SC radar. In service, the CXAM-1 was capable of detecting a large aircraft or aircraft formation flying at 10,000ft at 70 nautical miles or a small aircraft at 50 nautical miles.

US carrier air groups

The salient weakness of the US Navy's carrier force in 1942 was its difficulty in conducting coordinated air operations. This problem was already apparent at Coral Sea and reached new heights at Midway. Once a suitable target was located, existing doctrine called for each carrier to launch its entire air group, minus any fighters withheld for defense. Because the entire air group could not be accommodated in a single deckload, launching a large strike required two separate deckloads, making for a potentially long launch period as the first deckload waited overhead for the second deckload to be spotted and launched. Once launched, the different aircraft speeds and altitudes precluded a joint formation. Instead, the various squadrons would usually proceed together in loose order to the target, hopefully not losing contact with each other along the way. There was no attempt to coordinate multiple air groups from different carriers even if they were going after the same target.

Ideally, after approaching the target area, the dive-bomber and torpedo-bomber squadrons were in a position to launch a coordinated strike. This forced the enemy to split his defenses, which was an important consideration given the vulnerability of the torpedo planes. At Midway, only *Yorktown* was able to achieve any degree of coordinated strike. The failure of the other two air groups to achieve some degree of coordination meant that the vulnerable torpedo bombers attacked independently, with predictable results. The doctrine of independent strike by a single air group when combined with bad weather, poor communications, or bad navigation was a potential recipe for disappointment or even disaster. This was realized by *Hornet*'s strike on June 4 which was an unmitigated disaster and *Enterprise*'s which quickly fragmented. Only the courage and initiative of individual commanders compensated for this doctrinal weakness.

Complicating the task of American mission planners were the short ranges of their aircraft. In the strike role, the Dauntless dive-bomber had a maximum strike radius of up to 275 miles with a 500-pound bomb and some 200 miles with a full 1,000-pound bomb load. Torpedo bombers were limited to a range of 175 miles with a full torpedo load. The strike range of escorting fighters was limited to that of the torpedo bombers since no auxiliary fuel tanks were used at this point of the war.

Nimitz planned that the two carriers of Task Force 16 (TF-16) under Spruance would constitute the main strike force: both carriers would launch an all-out strike once the Japanese carriers were spotted. Task Force 17 (TF-17) under Fletcher, built around *Yorktown*, would serve as a search and reserve

A Dauntless of VB-3 aboard *Yorktown* warming up prior to launch on the morning of June 4. Aircraft from this squadron would account for *Soryu*. (US Naval Historical Center)

force to be employed at Fletcher's discretion. During the battle, Fletcher hedged his bets in order not to repeat the experience at Coral Sea, where he had launched a full strike from both his carriers at what turned out to be a secondary target. By keeping *Yorktown*'s Air Group in reserve, he would be ready to deal with any unexpected surprises.

Another lesson from Coral Sea was integrated into American planning for Midway. At Coral Sea, American fighters had been allocated half to combat air patrol and half to strike escort. After the power of Japanese naval aviation was amply demonstrated at Coral Sea, American fighter allocation was changed in favor of increased fleet air defense. At Midway, TF-16 allocated only ten fighters per carrier for strike escort; TF-17 dedicated only eight fighters for escort. Before Midway, the size of a fighter squadron was increased to 27 aircraft, made possible by the introduction of the F4F-4 with folding wings.

Each air group commander decided differently how to deal with the new fighter escort direction. Each of these different approaches had a real impact during the battle. *Hornet*'s Air Group was the least experienced. Mitscher decided that with only ten fighters he could not provide cover to both his dive-bomber and torpedo squadrons since each proceeded to the target at different altitudes. He also thought that the Wildcat needed a height advantage to deal with the faster Japanese "Zero" fighter. To maintain a height advantage, *Hornet*'s fighters were ordered to stay with the dive-bombers. The commander of *Hornet*'s torpedo squadron was justifiably concerned about the lack of direct fighter protection. *Hornet*'s Air Group would launch in two deckloads and proceed to the target in two separate groups. The dive-bombers would fly at an altitude of 20,000ft and were ordered to keep the torpedo bombers, flying at 1,500ft, in sight so that a coordinated strike could be executed. Further evidence of the inexperience of *Hornet*'s Air Group was the fact that the escort fighters were launched in the first deckload. Forced to wait for the entire strike to be launched and formed up, the result of this lack of caution to preserve the fuel of the short-legged fighters was disastrous.

Enterprise's more experienced air group decided on a different approach. Its strike was launched in two deckloads, but the escort fighters were part of the second deckload. All squadrons were ordered to fly within sight of one another so that a coordinated strike could be executed. The commander of the fighter squadron decided that the dive-bombers were more vulnerable; thus to provide direct support to them and to maintain an altitude advantage over defending Japanese fighters, he decided to keep his fighters at high altitude. He did promise the acting commander of the torpedo squadron that he would bring his fighters down to support the slow torpedo aircraft if required. *Yorktown*'s Air Group decided to send all eight of its fighters assigned to escort with the more vulnerable torpedo bombers.

US Navy June 1942 carrier air groups were composed of four squadrons. The fighter (actually called "fighting") squadron was equipped with 27 F4F Wildcat fighters. Two squadrons were equipped with the Douglas SBD Dauntless dive-bomber. One squadron was named a scouting squadron and the second a bombing squadron, though in practice both squadrons performed virtually identically. Dive-bombing squadrons possessed between 18 and 20 aircraft. The air group commander was usually assigned his own dive-bomber. The torpedo squadron was assigned 12–15 TBD Devastator aircraft. In the early war period, US Navy carriers each had a permanently assigned air group. Each of the assigned squadrons carried the hull number of the ship it was assigned to. For example, *Enterprise*'s fighter squadron was numbered VF-6, her dive-bombers VB-6, her scout bombers VS-6, and her torpedo squadron VT-6.

Yorktown's Air Group was reorganized after Coral Sea – the result of heavy losses and pilot exhaustion during the first six months of the war. VS-5 and VT-5 departed the Air Group and were replaced by VB-3 and VT-3 from *Saratoga*'s air group. Much to the displeasure of the squadron's pilots, VB-5 changed its name to VS-5 to avoid confusion with VB-3. VF-3 was also assigned to *Yorktown* to replace VF-42. VF-3 was reinforced with a nucleus of VF-42 pilots.

US carrier air defense

For the upcoming battle, and in accordance with existing doctrine, Nimitz decided to operate his carriers in two task forces. Prevailing doctrine called for carriers to operate in separate groups but close enough to be mutually supporting. The supposed advantage of this tactic was that if the groups were far enough away, then a single Japanese scout aircraft could not spot both groups. In reality, the dispersion tactic created more problems than it solved.

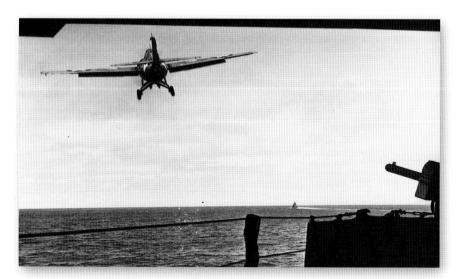

An F4F-4 Wildcat of VF-3 takes off from *Yorktown* to assume CAP duties on the morning of June 4. To the right is a .50-cal. machine gun. (US Naval Historical Center)

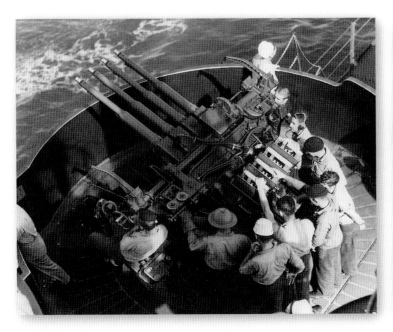

Since carriers did not operate that far apart, it usually did not prevent a single enemy scout aircraft from spotting both groups. Most importantly, dispersion increased the vulnerability of an individual carrier group to attack since it also dispersed available fighters and escorts. Dispersion also magnified the already considerable problems with strike coordination. At Coral Sea, Fletcher chose to operate both his carriers as a single formation. At Midway, Nimitz clearly ordered that separate carrier groups be maintained. Accordingly, Fletcher decided to separate his two task forces by 10–15 miles, close enough for mutual fighter support.

A single fighter controller on *Enterprise* would control all fighters. The key to successful fleet air defense was the integration of radar into the CAP allocation process. Despite the use of radar, real problems were evidenced at Coral Sea when the Japanese dive-bombers were allowed to strike their targets unmolested by friendly fighters. The fleet air-defense problem was better handled at Midway, but enough problems still existed to preclude truly effective fighter direction.

Augmenting the defensive efforts of the fighters were the antiaircraft guns aboard the carrier and its escorts. Unlike the IJN, the Americans placed their carriers inside a ring of escorts so that the inner escorts could provide their weight of antiaircraft fire to protect the carriers. US Navy carrier task groups maneuvered as a single entity under attack to keep formation and maximize antiaircraft protection to the carrier. American ships were equipped with some of the most effective antiaircraft weapons of the day. The standard long-range air-defense gun during 1942 was the 5in. dual-purpose gun. The 5in./38 gun was fitted aboard all three carriers and the escorting destroyers. It was an accurate gun and possessed a high rate of fire. The older 5in./25 gun aboard the escorting cruisers was still a capable weapon, but possessed a shorter range. Short-range antiaircraft protection was provided by the 1.1in. machine cannon. This was a four-barreled, water-cooled system that could deliver a rate of fire of 140 rounds per minute per barrel. However, in service it proved disappointing owing to continual jamming problems. Last-ditch air-defense protection was provided by .50-cal. machine guns and 20mm Oerlikon

LEFT
One of the 1.1in. gun mounts on board *Enterprise*. Each of the Yorktown-class carriers mounted four of these weapons at Midway, positioned fore and aft of the island. They were never popular in service because of jamming and maintenance problems. (US Naval Historical Center)

RIGHT
The after port side 5in. gun battery aboard *Enterprise*. Each Yorktown-class carrier mounted eight of these excellent weapons. (US Naval Historical Center)

LEFT
An SBD Dauntless from VB-6 returning to *Enterprise* following the attack on *Kaga* on the morning of June 4. The ability of the Dauntless to absorb damage, as shown here, combined with its excellence as an accurate bombing platform made it the outstanding weapon of the battle, accounting for all damage inflicted on the Japanese. (US Naval Historical Center)

RIGHT
This grainy photo shows a TBD Devastator taking off on June 4 to attack the 1st Kido Butai. The three torpedo squadrons launched 41 Devastators that day, but only six returned to their carriers. This was the Devastator's last combat action. (US Naval Historical Center)

automatic cannons. However, with an effective range of 2,000 yards or less, all these short-ranged weapons were usually unable to destroy Japanese aircraft before they dropped their weapons. Though American antiaircraft fire could not prevent an attack by skilled and determined Japanese aviators, it did take an increasingly significant toll on attacking Japanese aircraft.

Aircraft

The standard US Navy ship-borne fighter in June 1942 was the F4F "Wildcat." The F4F-4 had entered service in April 1942 and introduced improvements over previous models in armament and protection at the expense of performance. Experience at Coral Sea showed that the Wildcat was clearly outclassed in the areas of speed and maneuverability by the Japanese Zero fighter, but American pilots were already developing tactics to emphasize the Wildcat's advantages in firepower and protection.

The backbone of US carrier air groups was its two dive-bomber squadrons equipped with the Douglas SBD "Dauntless" dive-bomber. During a time when American carrier torpedo aircraft lacked an effective torpedo, the Dauntless constituted the striking power of the US Navy's carrier air groups. In June 1942, the SDB-3 was the primary model in service which mounted a dual machine gun for the rear gunner and carried improved armor and self-sealing fuel tanks. The Dauntless was a rugged aircraft able to absorb considerable combat damage, but it was most famous for being a stable and accurate bombing platform. Its only drawbacks were a mediocre top speed and non-folding wings that made movement and storage on carrier hangar and flight decks more difficult. In the hands of an experienced pilot, the Dauntless was a deadly weapon.

The final component of American carrier air groups was the TBD "Devastator." This obsolescent aircraft was slow and possessed a short combat radius. If this was not bad enough, the US Navy's aerial torpedo, the Mark XIII, was notoriously unreliable and could not be dropped above 100mph or above 120ft, making the Devastator exceedingly vulnerable in combat. The replacement for the Devastator, the TBF "Avenger," was just coming into service. Six of these aircraft were actually assigned to *Hornet*'s VT-8 during the battle, but were based on Midway.

Intelligence

Midway has often been described as a victory of intelligence. Without a doubt, American naval intelligence was a key advantage for Nimitz at Midway, but it was not a decisive advantage. It allowed Nimitz to position his forces to maximum benefit, but it did not mean that those forces were guaranteed success once the battle had been joined. The Americans had been making steady progress cracking the Japanese Navy code (known as JN-25B) since the start of the war. Real insights were not gained until April when advances allowed up to 85 percent of some signals to be read. This effort was made possible only by the delay in a scheduled Japanese Navy code change that was pushed back from April 1 to May 1, and finally late May.

It is generally believed that Nimitz had a full understanding of the Japanese forces involved in the operation and fully understood their plans. This was not the case, but the efforts of the American code breakers did provide him with a very good knowledge of the strength of Nagumo's carrier force, the invasion force and the Aleutians forces. However, Nimitz had no knowledge of Yamamoto's decision to employ his battleships assigned to the Main Body and the Guard Force. Nimitz did possess a basic understanding of the time lines of the Japanese operation. The rest was filled in by inspired analysis by him and his staff. The real value of this intelligence was that it gave enough confidence to Nimitz to believe and act upon the information he was receiving. In the case of Midway, unlike at Coral Sea where the intelligence provided to Fletcher was faulty with respect to the deployment of the Japanese carriers, the information provided to Nimitz at Midway was largely correct.

ORDERS OF BATTLE

All strengths shown are for June 4, 1942

IMPERIAL JAPANESE NAVY
MIDWAY FORCE

1st Kido Butai (Vice Admiral Nagumo Chuichi)

Carrier Division 1 (Vice Admiral Nagumo)

Carrier *Akagi* (Captain Aoki Taijiro)

Akagi Air Group (Commander Fuchida Mitsuo)

Akagi Carrier Fighter Unit	18 A6M2
Akagi Carrier Bomber Unit	18 D3A1
Akagi Carrier Attack Unit	18 B5N2
Total	54

Plus another six A6M2 from 6th Air Group

Carrier *Kaga* (Captain Okada Jisaku)

Kaga Air Group (Lieutenant Commander Kusumi Tadashi)

Kaga Carrier Fighter Unit	18 A6M2
Kaga Carrier Bomber Unit	18 D3A1
Kaga Carrier Attack Unit	27 B5N2
Total	63

Plus another nine A6M2 from 6th Air Group and possibly another two D3A1 aircraft from *Soryu*

Carrier Division 2 (Rear Admiral Yamaguchi Tamon)

Carrier *Hiryu* (Captain Kaku Tomeo)

Hiryu Air Group (Lieutenant Commander Tomonaga Joichi)

Hiryu Carrier Fighter Unit	18 A6M2
Hiryu Carrier Bomber Unit	18 D3A1
Hiryu Carrier Attack Unit	18 B5N2
Total	54

Plus another three A6M2 from 6th Air Group

Carrier *Soryu* (Captain Yanagimoto Ryusaku)

Soryu Air Group (Lieutenant Commander Egasa Takashige)

Soryu Carrier Fighter Unit	18 A6M2
Soryu Carrier Bomber Unit	16 D3A1
	1–2 D4Y1
Soryu Carrier Attack Unit	18 B5N2
Total	53–54

Plus another three A6M2 from 6th Air Group

Battleship Division 3, Section 2

Battleships *Haruna*, *Kirishima*

Cruiser Division 8

Heavy cruisers *Tone*, *Chikuma* (each with five search planes)

Destroyer Squadron 10

Light cruiser *Nagara* (Flagship)

Destroyer Division 4

Destroyers *Nowaki*, *Arashi*, *Hagikaze*, *Maikaze*

Destroyer Division 10

Destroyers *Kazagumo*, *Yugumo*, *Makigumo*

Destroyer Division 17

Destroyers *Urakaze*, *Isokaze*, *Tanikaze*, *Hamakaze*

Supply Group

Five oilers, Destroyer *Akigumo*

Main Body (Admiral Yamamoto Isoroku)

Battleship Division 1

Battleships *Yamato, Nagato, Mutsu*

Light carrier *Hosho* (8 B4Y1 Carrier Attack Aircraft)

Seaplane tenders *Chiyoda, Nisshin* (both carrying midget submarines for Midway)

Destroyer Squadron 3

Light cruiser *Sendai* (Flagship)

Destroyer Division 11

Destroyers *Fubuki, Shirayuki, Murakumo, Hatsuyuki*

Destroyer Division 19

Destroyers *Isonami, Uranami, Shikinami, Ayanami*

1st Supply Unit

Two oilers

Guard Force (Vice Admiral Takasu Shiro)

Battleship Division 2

Battleships *Ise, Hyuga, Fuso, Yamashiro*

Cruiser Division 9

Light cruisers *Oi, Kitakami*

Destroyer Division 20

Destroyers *Asagiri, Yugiri, Shirakumo, Amagiri*

Destroyer Division 24

Destroyers *Umikaze, Yamakaze, Kawakaze, Suzukaze*

Destroyer Division 27

Destroyers *Ariake, Yugure, Shigure, Shiratsuyu*

2nd Supply Unit

Two oilers

Midway Invasion Force (Vice Admiral Kondo Nobutake)

Light carrier *Zuiho*

Zuiho Air Group

Zuiho Carrier Fighter Unit	A6M2, 6 A5M4
Zuiho Carrier Attack Unit	12 B5N2
Total	24

Plane guard Destroyer *Mikazuki*

Battleship Division 3 (Section 1)

Battleships *Kongo, Hiei*

Cruiser Division 4 (Section 1)

Heavy cruisers *Atago, Chokai*

Cruiser Division 5

Heavy cruisers *Myoko, Haguro*

Destroyer Squadron 4

Light cruiser *Yura* (flagship)

Destroyer Division 3

Destroyers *Murasame, Samidare, Harusame, Yudachi*

Destroyer Division 9

Destroyers *Asagumo, Minegumo, Natsugumo*

Supply Group

Four oilers, Repair Ship *Akashi*

Close Support Group (Vice Admiral Kurita Takeo)

Cruiser Division 7

Heavy cruisers *Kumano, Suzuya, Mogami, Mikuma*

Destroyer Division 8

Destroyers *Arashio, Asashio*

One oiler

Transport Group (Rear Admiral Tanaka Raizo)

Destroyer Squadron 2

Light cruiser *Jintsu*

Destroyer Division 15

Destroyers *Kuroshio, Oyashio*

Destroyer Division 16

Destroyers *Yukikaze, Amatsukaze, Tokitsukaze, Hatsukaze*

Destroyer Division 18

Destroyers *Shiranuhi, Kasumi, Kagero, Arare*

Transports: 12

Patrol boats (old destroyers converted to carry troops) *1, 2, 34*

Oiler *Akebono Maru*

Seaplane Tender Group (Rear Admiral Fujita Ryutaro)

Seaplane tenders *Chitose* (20 aircraft) and *Kamikawa Maru* (12 aircraft)

Destroyer *Hayashio*

Patrol Boat *35* (old destroyer converted to carry troops)

Minesweeper Group

Four converted minesweepers

Three submarine chasers

Three supply/cargo ships

Advance Force (Submarines from 6th Fleet) (Vice Admiral Komatsu Teruhishi)

Submarine Squadron 3

Submarines *I-168, I-169, I-171, I-174, I-175*

Submarine Squadron 5

Submarine Division 19

Submarines *I-156, I-157, I-158, I-159*

Submarine Division 30

Submarines *I-162, I-165, I-166*

Submarine Division 13 (assigned to support Operation *K*)

Submarines *I-121, I-122, I-123*

Land-based Air Force

11th Air Fleet (Vice Admiral Tsukahara Nishizo at Tinian)

Midway Expeditionary Force

36 A6M2 fighters (carried aboard carriers of 1st and 2nd Kido Butai)

Ten land-based bombers (based at Wake Island)

Six flying boats (based at Jaluit Island)

24th Air Flotilla

Chitose Air Group (based at Kwajalein Island)
   36 A6M2 fighters
   36 land-based bombers
1st Air Group (based at Aur and Wotje Islands)
   36 A6M2 fighters
   36 land-based bombers
14th Air Group (based at Jaluit and Wotje Islands)
   18 flying boats

ALEUTIANS FORCE

2nd Kido Butai (Rear Admiral Kakuta Kakuji)
Carrier Division 4
Light carrier *Ryujo*
Ryujo Air Group

Ryujo Carrier Fighter Unit	12 A6M2	
Ryujo Carrier Attack Unit	18 B5N1/2	
Total	30	

Light carrier *Junyo*
Junyo Air Group

Junyo Carrier Fighter Unit	18 A6M2	
Junyo Carrier Bomber Unit	15 D3A1	
Total	33	

Cruiser Division 4 (Section 2)
   Heavy cruisers *Maya*, *Takao*
Destroyer Division 7
   Destroyers *Akebono*, *Ushio*, *Sazanami*
One oiler

Main Body (Vice Admiral Hosogaya Moshiro)
Heavy cruiser *Nachi*
Destroyers *Ikazuchi*, *Inazuma*
Two oilers
Three cargo ships

Attu-Adak Invasion Force (Rear Admiral Omori Sentaro)
Light cruiser *Abukuma*
Destroyer Division 21
   Destroyers *Wakaba*, *Nenohi*, *Hatsushimo*, *Hatsuhara*
One minelayer
One troop transport

Kiska Invasion Force (Captain Ono Takeji)
Cruiser Division 21
Light cruisers *Kiso*, *Tama*, 2 auxiliary cruisers
Destroyer Division 6
   Destroyers *Hibiki*, *Akatsuki*, *Hokaze*
Two troop transport
Three converted minesweepers

Seaplane Tender Force (Captain Ujuku Keiichi)
Seaplane tender *Kimikawa Maru* (8 aircraft)
Destroyer *Shiokaze*

Submarine Detachment (Rear Admiral Yamazaki Shigeaki)
Submarine Squadron 1
   Submarine *I-9*
   Submarine Division 2
      Submarines *I-15*, *I-17*, *I-19*
   Submarine Division 4
      Submarines *I-25*, *I-26*

US FORCES
TASK FORCE 17 (REAR ADMIRAL FRANK JACK FLETCHER)
Carrier Group Task Group 17.5
Yorktown (Captain Elliott Buckmaster)
Yorktown Air Group (Lieutenant Commander Oscar Perderson)
   Fighting Three (Lieutenant Commander John Thatch)
      25 F4F-4
   Bombing Three (Lieutenant Commander Maxwell Leslie)
      18 SBD-3
   Scouting Five (Lieutenant Wallace Short)
      19 SBD-3
   Torpedo Five (Lieutenant Commander Lance Massey)
      13 TBD-1
   Total   75
Cruiser Group Task Group 17.2
   Heavy cruisers *Astoria*, *Portland*
Destroyer Screen Task Group 17.4
   Destroyers *Morris*, *Anderson*, *Hammann*, *Russell*, *Hughes*, *Gwin*

TASK FORCE 16 (REAR ADMIRAL RAYMOND SPRUANCE)
Carrier Group Task Group 16.5
Enterprise (Captain George Murray)
Enterprise Air Group (Lieutenant Commander Clarence McClusky)
   Fighting Six (Lieutenant James Gray)
      27 F4F-4
   Bombing Six (Lieutenant Richard Best)
      19 SBD-2/3
   Scouting Six (Lieutenant Wilmer Gallaher)
      19 SBD-2/3
   Torpedo Six (Lieutenant Commander Eugene Lindsey)
      14 TBD-1
   Total   79
Hornet (Captain Marc Mitscher)
Hornet Air Group (Commander Stanhope Ring)
   Fighting Eight (Lieutenant Commander Samuel Mitchell)
      27 F4F-4
   Bombing Eight (Lieutenant Commander Robert Johnson)
      19 SBD-2/3
   Scouting Eight (Lieutenant Commander Walter Rodee)
      18 SBD-1/2/3

Torpedo Eight (Lieutenant Commander John Waldron)

              15 TBD-1

Total   79

Cruiser Group Task Group 16.2

Heavy cruiser *Minneapolis, New Orleans, Vincennes, Northampton, Pensacola*

Light cruiser *Atlanta*

Destroyer Screen Task Group 16.4

Destroyers *Phelps, Alywin, Monaghan, Worden, Balch, Conyngham, Benham, Ellet, Maury*

Oiler Group

Oilers *Cimarron, Platte*

Destroyers *Dewey, Monssen*

SUBMARINE FORCE (REAR ADMIRAL ROBERT ENGLISH)

Task Group 7.1 Midway Patrol Group

Submarines *Cachalot, Flying Fish, Tambor, Trout, Grayling, Nautilus, Grouper, Dolphin, Gato, Cuttlefish, Gudgeon, Grenadier*

Task Force 7.2 "Roving Short-stops"

Submarines *Narwhal, Plunger, Trigger*

Task Force 7.3 North of Oahu

Submarines *Tarpon, Pike, Finback, Growler*

Hawaiian Sea Frontier

Deployed at French Frigate Shoals

    Destroyer *Clark*

    Seaplane Tenders *Ballard, Thornton*

Deployed at Pearl and Hermes Reef

    Oiler *Kaloli*

    Minesweeper/Tug *Vireo*

    Converted yacht *Crystal*

Deployed at Lisianski, Gardner Pinnacles, Laysan and Necker

    4 Patrol boats

Midway Relief Fueling Unit

Oiler *Guadalupe*

Destroyers *Blue, Ralph Talbot*

MIDWAY ATOLL GARRISON (CAPTAIN CYRIL SIMARD)

Midway Naval Air Station (Captain Simard)

Marine Aircraft Group 22 (Lieutenant Colonel Ira Kimes)

VMF-211	21 F2A-3 Buffalo (20 operational, June 4)	
	7 F4F-3 Wildcat (6 operational)	
VMSB-241	19 SBD-2 Dauntless (18 operational)	
	21 SB2U-3 Vindicator (14 operational)	

VT-8 (Detachment)   6 TBF-1 Avenger (6 operational)

Patrol Squadron (VP) 24   6 PBY-5A (6 operational)

VP-44   8 PBY-5A (7 operational)

VP-51   3 PBY-5A (3 operational)

United States Army Air Corps VII Army Air Force Detachment

22nd and 69th Bombardment Squadrons (Medium)   4 B-26 Marauder (4 operational)

31st, 42nd, 72nd, 431st Bombardment Squadrons (Heavy) and 7th Air Force Headquarters

        16 B-17E Flying Fortress (14 operational)

349th Bombardment Squadron (Heavy)   1 B-17D

(1 operational)

Sand Island Seaplane Base

VP-23   14 PBY-5 (13 operational)

Midway Local Defenses

6th Marine Defense Battalion (reinforced with elements of the Third Marine Defense Battalion and two companies from 2nd Raider Battalion)

Total strength of garrison: 3,652 personnel

Motor Torpedo Boat Squadron 1

10 PT Boats, 4 Patrol Craft

ALEUTIANS FORCES

Task Group 8 (Rear Admiral Robert Theobald)

Heavy cruisers *Indianapolis, Louisville*

Light cruisers *Nashville, St. Louis, Honolulu*

Destroyer Division 11

    Destroyers *Gridley, McCall, Gilmer, Humphreys*

Destroyer Striking Group (Commander Wyatt Craig)

Destroyers *Case, Reid, Brooks, Sands, Kane, Dent, Talbot, King, Waters*

Submarine Group (Commander Burton Lake)

Submarines *S-18, S-23, S-27, S-28, S-35*

Tanker Group (Captain Houston Maples)

Tankers *Sabine, Brazos*

Transport *Comet*

OPPOSING PLANS

THE JAPANESE PLAN: YAMAMOTO GETS HIS WAY

The preparation of the plans for Midway by the Japanese is a textbook example of how not to plan a major operation. The strategic guidance for the operation was the result of a compromise between the Combined Fleet and the Naval General Staff. Even worse than the strategic planning, bad as that was, was the sloppy and flawed operational planning by the staff of the Combined Fleet which gave the Americans the opportunity to defeat the larger Japanese fleet in detail. On balance, the entire planning process reflected very poorly on the Japanese.

The initial period of the war had achieved all the aims of the Japanese with minimal losses. By April, all the objectives of the so-called First Operational Stage had been met or were close to being met. It was at this point that the Japanese began to diverge on the future scope of planning. The Second Operational Phase would expand Japan's strategic depth by adding eastern New Guinea, New Britain, the Aleutians, Midway, the Fijis, Samoa, and "strategic points in the Australian area." However, the Combined Fleet and the Naval General Staff led by Admiral Nagano Osami, had different views on the phasing of the Second Operational Phase objectives. The Naval General Staff favored an advance to the south to seize parts of Australia. This objective was quickly vetoed by the Imperial Japanese Army (IJA) which lacked sufficient troops for such an ambitious undertaking. Failing this, the Naval General Staff still advocated cutting the sea links between Australia and the United States. This could be accomplished by capturing New Caledonia, Fiji, and Samoa. This less ambitious operation required minimal ground resources and was favored by the Army. By March 13, the Naval General Staff and the Army had agreed to mount operations with the goal of capturing Fiji and Samoa.

Meanwhile, early Japanese moves in the South Pacific had brought an American response. On March 10, two American carriers attacked the Japanese invasion force after it had seized Lae and Salamaua on the New Guinea coast. The strength of the American response made the Japanese put on hold all future aggressive moves in the South Pacific until some of the IJN's carriers could be dispatched to the area to provide cover.

Despite the chain of events in the South Pacific, which seemed to rivet Japanese attention, and the apparent agreement in Tokyo between the IJA and IJN to push further south, Yamamoto and the staff of the Combined Fleet refused to be sidelined when it came to the formulation of Japanese naval

Admiral Nagano Osami was head of the Naval General Staff. From the Pearl Harbor attack until Midway, he differed on strategy with the Commander of the Combined Fleet, Admiral Yamamoto Isoroku. By May 1942, Nagano's influence was waning and Yamamoto was ascendant in the formulation of Japanese naval strategy. (US Naval Historical Center)

Midway is composed of two islands. Eastern Island in the foreground contains the airfield, and Sand Island, across the channel, was home to a seaplane base. Midway was the lure used by Yamamoto to force the Pacific Fleet to confront the assembled might of the Combined Fleet. (US Naval Historical Center)

strategy. In Yamamoto's view, the essential requirement for victory was to complete the destruction of the US Navy's Pacific Fleet. To accomplish this, Yamamoto needed to attack a target that the Pacific Fleet could not afford to lose. The obvious choice was Hawaii, but its large garrison and land-based air force made it impossible to attack and invade. Just as good, Yamamoto thought, was Midway Atoll. It was close enough to Hawaii that the Pacific Fleet would be compelled to fight for it, but far enough away so that Hawaii's land-based air power could play no role in the battle.

The issue came to a head during a meeting in Tokyo on April 2–5 between the Navy General Staff and representatives of the Combined Fleet. The Navy General Staff pointed out the limited utility of Midway as a base to threaten Hawaii as well as the enormous difficulties in supplying a base so close to the main American base at Pearl Harbor.

Yamamoto refused to budge in the face of whatever logic the Navy General Staff could muster, and by April 5 got his way. As he had done before Pearl Harbor, an implied threat of resignation allowed him to hijack the formulation of Japanese naval strategy. However, his victory was incomplete. In exchange for his desired Midway operation, Yamamoto had to agree to two demands from the Naval General Staff. Both of these directly compromised the success of the Midway operation, demonstrating as nothing else could the bankruptcy of Japanese naval planning. To get the advance in the South Pacific back on track, Yamamoto agreed to send part of his carrier force to protect the projected early May invasion of Port Moresby. Further dissipating Japanese naval assets, Yamamoto agreed to include an attack to seize selected points in the Aleutians concurrent with the Midway operation. Yamamoto's overconfidence led him to believe that he had enough strength to conduct both operations at once.

Operation *MI* in detail

The Japanese plan for Operation *MI* was deeply flawed. However, these flaws are easily understood once the assumptions Yamamoto used for planning are outlined. Unfortunately for the Japanese, these assumptions exhibited almost no insight into how the Americans planned to fight the battle. Despite his revolutionary use of naval airpower for the first few months of the war, the anticipation of a decisive clash with the US Pacific Fleet provided Yamamoto with the intellectual background for reversion to a set-piece battle much like the battle the Japanese had been planning to fight for many years before the war in the Western Pacific against the US Navy.

Operation *MI* was scheduled to open on the morning of June 3 with a devastating blow by Nagumo's carrier force against Midway. Nagumo's force of six carriers escorted by two battleships, two heavy cruisers, one light cruiser, and 11 destroyers (the same force employed to strike Pearl Harbor) would approach Midway from the northwest to knock out its air strength in a single blow. Of course, as at Pearl Harbor, strategic and tactical surprise was assumed. Further air strikes were envisioned on Midway on June 4 preparatory to a landing. On June 5, the Seaplane Tender Group would land on Kure Island 60 miles west of Midway to set up a seaplane base.

All of this was a prelude to the landing on Midway Atoll scheduled for June 6. A Transport Group with 12 transports and three patrol boats (converted destroyers designed to land troops) escorted by one light cruiser and 10 destroyers was to deliver a total of 5,000 troops. The Second Combined Special Naval Landing Force of some 1,500 men was allocated against Sand Island while the IJA's Ichiki Detachment (named after Colonel Ichiki Kiyonao) with a 1,000-man reinforced battalion was dedicated to Eastern Island. Both forces were to be landed by barge on the southern shores of their objectives where the reef was less of an obstacle. Several other groups supported the invasion including the Close Support Group of four heavy cruisers and two destroyers, a minesweeper group, and the Invasion Force Main Body with two battleships, another four heavy cruisers, eight destroyers, and a light carrier.

Following the expected quick capture of the island, two construction battalions were tasked to quickly make the base operational. To accomplish this before the expected clash with the American fleet, they were given exactly one day. The base would become a veritable fortress with the fighters from Nagumo's carriers as well as six Type A midget submarines, five motor torpedo boats, 94 cannon, and 40 machine guns carried aboard the transports.

The seizure of Midway was only the prelude to the most important part of the Japanese objective. The entire premise of Yamamoto's plan was that an attack on Midway would force the American Pacific Fleet into battle, and that Yamamoto would have adequate time to prepare a trap for the Americans after they recovered from the surprise of the Japanese attack and sortied from Pearl Harbor. Another major assumption was that the operation would gain strategic surprise and the US Pacific Fleet would need three days to sortie from Pearl Harbor to Midway to offer battle. However, Yamamoto was concerned that an overwhelming show of force on the part of the Combined Fleet could

An overhead view of the heavy cruiser *Tone* in 1941. The class was designed with its entire main battery forward in order to maximize the space aft for aviation facilities. The two cruisers of the *Tone* class were assigned to the 1st Kido Butai from the outbreak of war up through Midway. (Yamato Museum)

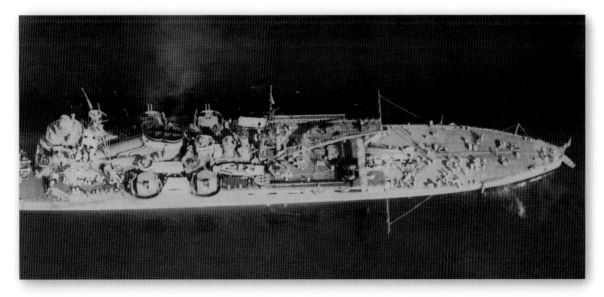

make the Americans think twice about giving battle at all. This concern does much to explain Yamamoto's dispersal of forces. His disposition was a deception that would prevent the Americans from gauging his true strength and thereby convince the Americans that conditions were suitable for a major engagement. When the Pacific Fleet made an appearance, the many parts of the Combined Fleet would converge to crush the Americans.

After Midway was captured, Nagumo would take his carriers some 500 miles to the northeast of the island. The Invasion Force would remain near Midway as apparent bait to induce the Americans to leave Pearl Harbor. The other Japanese heavy forces would linger to the north, out of range of American reconnaissance. The Main Body would be positioned some 300 miles to the west of Nagumo's force, and the other battleship force, the Guard Force, would move to a position some 500 miles north of the Main Body. Meanwhile, the carriers from the 2nd Kido Butai would also move south from the Aleutians and linger some 300 miles to the east of the Guard Force.

In this scenario, once the Japanese were positioned, the Pacific Fleet would make an appearance to hit the Invasion Force as it patrolled near Midway. Perhaps most bizarrely, the Japanese appear to have believed that the Pacific Fleet's response would include not only the remaining American carriers, but also the Pacific Fleet's remaining battleships. In a page from the finely scripted Japanese prewar plans for a decisive clash, submarines and aircraft would strike the American Fleet, causing great attrition. The final blow would be delivered by the massed Japanese battleships, now concentrated to finish off the Americans.

Another component of the Japanese plan called for the employment of a large number of submarines. When this part of the plan is examined, it provides further evidence of sloppy thinking combined with sheer arrogance. Two picket lines of submarines were stationed on what the Japanese believed would be the route of the American advance from Pearl Harbor to Midway. Each was composed of seven large submarines assigned to a patrol box. This deployment was faulty as there was space between each patrol box for the Americans to steam through undetected. The submarines assigned to this duty were not even the Combined Fleet's most modern units, but instead were older units which had maintenance problems. Worst of all, because of delays in leaving their bases, the submarines would not even reach their stations until as late as June 3, after the American carriers had already passed through. Another planned operation involving submarines was also unsuccessful. In order to gain intelligence on the location of Pacific Fleet units at Pearl Harbor, the Japanese planned to use a large flying boat operating from the islands of Jaluit and Wotje to surveil the base on May 31. To reach Pearl Harbor, the flying boats had to refuel en route. The plan was for tanker submarines to meet the flying boats at an uninhabited islet called the French Frigate Shoals which was located between Midway and Hawaii. The entire operation was codenamed Operation *K*. Because the concept had been used twice before, and the repeat operation had been disclosed to the Americans by broken codes, American units were assigned to patrol the French Frigate Shoals. Thus, Yamamoto received none of the expected advance warning of American fleet movements from his submarines.

One of the most misunderstood aspects of the Midway plan was Operation *AL*, the plan to seize two islands of the Aleutian chain. It is commonly believed that the Aleutian operation was a diversion to draw American forces from the defense of Midway; however, Japanese sources never mention any diversionary aspect to the Aleutian landings. These were to be conducted simultaneously with the Midway landings. Belief that the Aleutians landings were a diversion does not even pass the common-sense test when examined in the overall context of Yamamoto's desire to crush the US Pacific Fleet. Even if Nimitz felt compelled to commit a significant portion of his forces to defend the Aleutians, in itself highly unlikely, the last thing Yamamoto wanted was a diversion that drew forces north away from his elaborate trap off Midway.

Operation *AL* called for a carrier strike against the US naval base at Dutch Harbor on June 3, the same day as the originally scheduled strike on Midway. Landings on the islands of Kiska and Adak were scheduled for June 6. The Adak landing was actually a temporary measure to allow the destruction of the US facility thought to be there. Another optional landing was planned on Attu on June 12.

Yamamoto devoted considerable forces to conduct Operation *AL*. The most powerful elements were the two carriers of the 2nd Kido Butai, *Junyo* and *Ryujo*. These were escorted by two heavy cruisers and three destroyers and supported by an oiler. While the two carriers assigned to this operation were clearly second-line units, their total of 63 embarked aircraft made them equal to one of Nagumo's fleet carriers. The entire operation was commanded by Vice Admiral Hosogaya Moshiro who also exercised direct control of the Northern Force Main Body with another heavy cruiser and two destroyers. The Invasion Force was divided into two sections with a total of three transports escorted by three light cruisers, seven destroyers, and other auxiliaries. Army troops were tasked to seize Adak and Attu and a Special Naval Landing Force, along with a construction battalion, was allocated to take Kiska.

Providing distant cover for Operation *AL* was the Guard Force which was positioned to intervene if required. This force contained four battleships, two light cruisers and 12 destroyers supported by two oilers.

Vice Admiral Hosogaya Moshiro exercised overall command of the Aleutians operations. The considerable forces placed under his command were too distant to contribute to the main battle fought at Midway. (US Naval Historical Center)

All considered, Operation *AL* was the best demonstration of Yamamoto's flawed objective prioritization and faulty force allocation. The Aleutians were clearly a secondary objective unworthy of the forces dedicated to seize them. If Operation *MI* was planned to be the decisive battle, any diversion of forces violated the principle of mass and was unwise. If the Midway operation went well and resulted in the crippling of the American fleet, the Aleutians could be seized at Yamamoto's leisure. If the Midway operation was a failure, any gains made in the Aleutians could not ultimately be held anyway, as was proven later in 1943. Any forces sent north to conduct Operation *AL* were in no position to support Operation *MI*, and were thus essentially worthless in any clash with the US Pacific Fleet.

It is hard to know where to start when providing a critique of the plan for Operation *MI*. The planning process was riddled with flawed assumptions, a total disregard for the enemy, and obviously contained more than a little arrogance. As was common in Japanese naval planning, the operation was complex. In the case of the Midway operation, Yamamoto had 12 different forces spread out over a large chunk of the Pacific Ocean. This complexity was a hallmark of Japanese naval planning, but Yamamoto seems to have delighted in taking this to new heights. It violated the principle of concentration and reduced the chances of successful coordination among the far-flung groups. Each of the main groups was deployed too far away from each other to be mutually supporting.

The most damning aspect of the plan was the determination by the Japanese to squander their considerable numerical advantage over the American Pacific Fleet. This process, begun at Coral Sea a month earlier, reached its zenith in June 1942. Operation *AL* took 50 ships into a strategic deadend. Most of Yamamoto's heavy forces were deployed so far to the rear that they were irrelevant to the outcome of the battle. Defenders of Yamamoto would point out that his primary concern was not whether the Pacific Fleet could be crushed but whether it would come out of Pearl Harbor to be engaged at all. Deployment of his forces must be seen in that light, explaining the dispersion of forces in order not to scare the Americans out of a fight. However, there was no way that such a large operation could be deceptive and mutually supporting, and given a choice, Yamamoto had to choose the latter. The result was that the Japanese were actually outnumbered at the point of contact where the battle would be decided. Nimitz's force of 26 ships faced a force of 20 ships of the 1st Kido Butai with an aircraft count of 233 (348 if Midway is included) against Nagumo's 248.

Yamamoto's plan was driven by a series of flawed assumptions, instead of planning for the most dangerous course of action open to the enemy. His biggest assumption was in fact correct: the Americans were prepared to fight for Midway. But his assumptions on how they would conduct that fight were entirely wrong. The assumption that the operation would gain strategic and tactical surprise was disastrously wrong. The role of overconfidence also cannot be overlooked in Japanese planning. The unbroken run of success since the opening of the war resulted in the so-called "victory disease" rearing its head in the planning process. This allowed the Japanese to overlook many of the shortcomings of the Midway operation and meant that when Carrier Division 5 was removed from the IJN's order of battle after the Coral Sea operation, the Kido Butai's four remaining carriers were still seen as more than enough. It meant that two carriers could be sent to participate in the meaningless Aleutians operation. It meant that the inadequate pre-battle reconnaissance was viewed as unimportant. It meant that even after the Kido Butai had to postpone sailing by one day, Yamamoto did not see fit to make any adjustments to his plan.

THE US PLAN

Despite popular myth, Nimitz's decision to engage the Japanese at Midway was not a desperate gamble against impossible odds but a carefully calculated plan with great potential to cause serious damage to the enemy. The battle was clearly Nimitz's; he would retain "grand tactical control" from Hawaii.

The basis for Nimitz's planning for the Midway battle (contained in Cincpac Operation Plan 29-42) was his high degree of insight into Japanese intentions and strength. However, Nimitz did not have the degree of insight into specific Japanese plans that is commonly believed. The Pacific Fleet's cryptologists had assembled a fairly close idea of the IJN's intentions. The main target of the operation was identified as Midway, where four–five large carriers, two–four fast battleships, seven–nine heavy cruisers, escorted by a commensurate number of destroyers, up to 24 submarines and a landing force, could be expected. Additional forces, including carriers would be dedicated against the Aleutians. The operation would be conducted during the first week of June, but the precise timing remained unclear. Nimitz believed that June 5 was the day scheduled for simultaneous landings on Midway and the Aleutians. The landing would be preceded by air attack from Japanese carriers, expected on June 3 or 4, and by heavy bombardment by surface ships at night. Submarines would support the operation by trying to attack American ships headed from Pearl Harbor to Midway and flying boats would repeat the March night bombing of Pearl Harbor. All in all, this was a fairly close approximation to Japanese plans, but somewhat lacking in specifics.

To engage the Japanese, Nimitz carefully arrayed his available assets. Unfortunately for Yamamoto, his plans were nothing like the Japanese assumed. Despite the constant suggestions from US Navy Commander Admiral Ernest King that they be employed as aggressively as possible, Nimitz immediately decided that there was no place for the Pacific Fleet's seven remaining battleships. He did not want his carriers to be hamstrung in any way by the slow battleships and, besides, he had no assets available to provide them adequate air cover or screening. The battleships remained out of harm's way in San Francisco.

LEFT
Astoria was one of seven *New Orleans*-class heavy cruisers. With a top speed of 33 knots and a fairly heavy antiaircraft armament (for 1942) of eight 5in. guns and four 1.1in. mounts, these ships were well suited to act as carrier escorts. *Astoria* was assigned to TF-17 and acted as Fletcher's flagship after he was forced to leave the damaged *Yorktown*. (US Naval Historical Center)

RIGHT
A US Army Air Force B-17 "Flying Fortress" takes off from Midway to bomb the Japanese fleet during the battle. Despite the claims of the Air Corps aviators, the B-17s failed to score a single hit during the battle. (US Naval Historical Center)

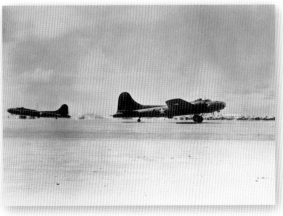

The Pacific Fleet's striking power resided in its carriers. Two of these, *Enterprise* and *Hornet*, were assigned to Spruance as TF-16 and would be off Midway by June 1. The damaged *Yorktown*, still in TF-17, remained as Fletcher's flagship and would be in position off Midway by June 2. Fletcher would assume overall command of the two carrier groups when he arrived.

Nimitz held a major advantage in that the battle was being fought within range of friendly aircraft. Midway was jammed with as many aircraft as possible, including a large number of long-range reconnaissance aircraft, fighters to defend the base from air attack, and a mixed strike force of Marine, Navy and Army Air Corps aircraft. Defending the base were a number of submarines and a garrison of some 2,000 Marines.

Employment of Midway's 115 aircraft was an important consideration. Most important was the employment of the long-range PBY flying boats. Nimitz had some indication that the Japanese air strikes on the island would occur from short range, probably from the northwest. Within that framework, Nimitz put much thought into the deployment of his carriers and analyzed the best position for them to minimize their risk and yet be well placed to deal punishing blows to the Japanese carriers as they attacked Midway. The key was the availability of scouting support from Midway, which was tasked to conduct searches out to 700 miles, greatly reducing the possibility of a surprise air raid on the island. Nimitz agreed with his staff that the best position for the carriers was northeast of Midway. By being fairly close to Midway, they could respond quickly to attacking enemy carriers.

Most important was the question of risk to the carriers. Nimitz never saw the battle as a death-struggle for control of Midway. His orders to Fletcher and Spruance provided the guidance that they were to "be governed by the principle of calculated risk which you shall interpret to mean the avoidance of exposure of your forces to attack by superior enemy forces without good prospect of inflicting, as a result of such exposure, greater damage to the enemy." On top of these written orders, Nimitz personally instructed Spruance not to lose his carriers no matter what. If required, he was to abandon Midway and let the Japanese attempt a landing. Even if captured, it could be recaptured later. It must be assumed that Nimitz provided the same instruction to Fletcher.

Eventually, Nimitz decided on the specific point where he wanted his carriers to linger – so-called "Point Luck" 325 miles northeast of Midway. The last intelligence provided by Nimitz to his carrier commanders provided an almost precise assessment of Nagumo's force – four carriers, two battleships, two heavy cruisers, and 12 destroyers. Nimitz believed that these carriers would be operated in two separate groups, each with two carriers, one likely attacking Midway and the other providing cover. Nimitz held high hopes that his carriers could ambush the Japanese carriers attacking Midway, followed by a second phase where three American carriers faced just two Japanese.

THE BATTLE OF MIDWAY

OPENING MOVES

On May 27, the 1st Kido Butai departed Hashirajima Anchorage located in the Inland Sea in Hiroshima Bay. This was one day later than scheduled. However, with the landing day on Midway determined by tidal conditions, the overall plan was not modified. This meant one day less was available to neutralize Midway before the scheduled landing.

Another aspect of the tightly synchronized Japanese plan was also falling behind schedule. The submarines for the scouting cordon were late leaving Kwajalein between May 26 and 30. Some arrived on station on June 3, not June 1 as planned. By this time the American carriers had already moved through the area. The commander of the 6th Fleet did not even think it was important enough to tell Yamamoto of this fact. On May 31, Operation *K* was abandoned when submarine *I-121* approached the French Frigate Shoals and found American ships present.

Meanwhile, other signs pointed to increased American awareness that something was brewing. Submarine *I-168* conducted a reconnaissance of Midway on June 2 and reported heavy air activity from the island during the day and work continuing at night. Japanese traffic analysis had noted an increase in American naval radio traffic with many messages marked as "urgent." Based on this, the analysis followed that the Pacific Fleet was not sitting idly in Pearl Harbor. Again, these developments did not prompt the Japanese to alter their plans.

Hiryu shown at speed in 1939. *Hiryu* was an improved, larger version of *Soryu*. In late April 1942, the commander of Carrier Division 2, Rear Admiral Yamaguchi, moved his flag from *Soryu* to *Hiryu* to take advantage of the larger bridge on *Hiryu*. (Yamato Museum)

The Central Pacific showing Midway and the approach to contact by forces of both sides, June 1–3

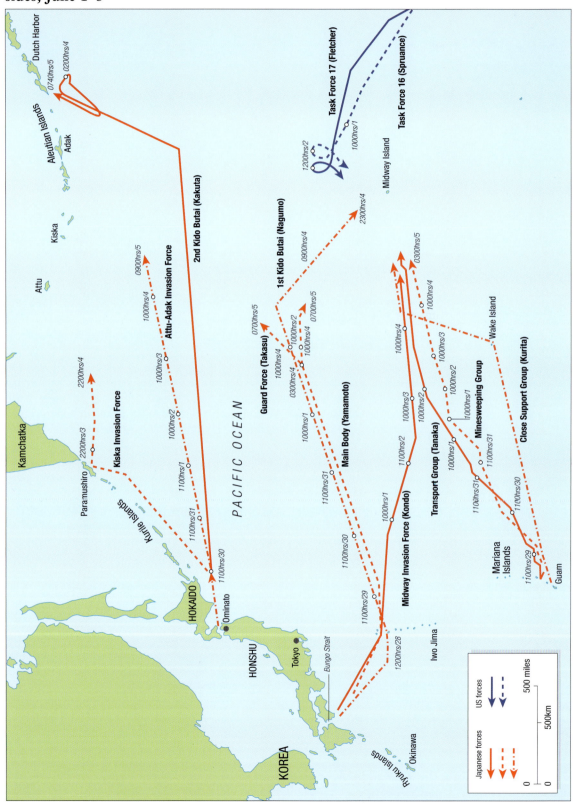

Dutch Harbor
0200hrs/4
0740hrs/5
Aleutian Islands
Adak
Kiska
Attu
2nd Kido Butai (Kakuta)
Attu-Adak Invasion Force
0900hrs/5
1000hrs/4
1000hrs/3
1000hrs/2
1100hrs/1
1100hrs/31
Kamchatka
2200hrs/4
2200hrs/3
Kiska Invasion Force
Paramushiro
Kurile Islands
1100hrs/31
1100hrs/30
Ominato
HOKAIDO
HONSHU
Tokyo
Bungo Strait
Iwo Jima
KOREA
Ryuku Islands
Okinawa

PACIFIC OCEAN

Task Force 17 (Fletcher)
Task Force 16 (Spruance)
1200hrs/2
1000hrs/1
Midway Island

1st Kido Butai (Nagumo)
2300hrs/4
0900hrs/4
0700hrs/5
Guard Force (Takasu)
0700hrs/5
1000hrs/4
0300hrs/4
1000hrs/2
1000hrs/4
0700hrs/5
1000hrs/1
Main Body (Yamamoto)
1100hrs/31
1100hrs/30
1100hrs/29
1200hrs/28
Midway Invasion Force (Kondo)
1000hrs/1
1100hrs/2
1000hrs/3
1000hrs/2
1000hrs/4
0300hrs/5
Transport Group (Tanaka)
1000hrs/4
1000hrs/3
1000hrs/2
1000hrs/1
1100hrs/31
Minesweeping Group
1100hrs/31
Close Support Group (Kurita)
Wake Island
1100hrs/30
1100hrs/29
Guam
Mariana Islands

Japanese forces
US forces
500 miles
500km
0
0

42

Carriers *Hornet* and *Enterprise* arrived in Pearl Harbor on May 26 following their brief South Pacific deployment. *Yorktown* arrived in Pearl Harbor on May 27 and went into dry dock the next morning to repair her Coral Sea battle damage. *Hornet* and *Enterprise* sortied on May 28. *Yorktown* was out of dry dock on May 29 and departed the next day to join her sister ships.

After leaving Pearl Harbor, TF-16 steered to the northwest to take its assigned position 350 miles northeast of Midway. TF-16 rendezvoused with *Yorktown* on June 2 at 1600hrs 325 miles northeast of Midway. At this point, Fletcher assumed command. The assembled strength of the US Pacific Fleet, three carriers, eight cruisers, and 15 destroyers, now waited to combat the combined might of the IJN.

On the morning of June 3, *Yorktown* launched 20 Dauntlesses to conduct searches. Fletcher moved his carriers to a new position some 175 miles west of Point Luck in anticipation of a Japanese attack on Midway. Meanwhile, the 1st Kido Butai approached Midway from the north where the weather was very bad on June 2 and 3.

Though the Japanese plan had called for the battle to open with a surprise air attack on Midway, Nagumo's late departure meant that the first Japanese force to be spotted was the Invasion Force which continued to close on Midway on schedule and was already in range of Midway's air searches. At 0843hrs on the morning of June 3, PBYs from Midway spotted the Minesweeper Group. Less than an hour later, PBYs spotted the Transport Group approximately 700 miles west of Midway. This was incorrectly identified as "Main Body." The first attack of the battle was delivered by nine B-17s from the 431st Bombardment Squadron which departed Midway after 1200hrs to strike the Japanese transports. Though no hits were scored, the Japanese could not remain under the illusion that strategic surprise was still possible.

The B-17 attack was followed by another strike on the Transport Group early on June 4. Four radar-equipped PBYs were rigged to conduct a night torpedo attack. One aborted owing to bad weather, but the other three pressed on to arrive in the area of the invasion convoy at about 0130hrs. The first two aircraft missed, but the third placed a torpedo into tanker *Akebono Maru* killing 23 crewmen. The tanker was able to continue in formation.

THE JAPANESE STRIKE MIDWAY

At 0430hrs on June 4, Nagumo started launching 108 aircraft to strike Midway. The strike was composed of 18 carrier bombers from *Akagi* and *Kaga* and 18 carrier attack planes from *Soryu* and *Hiryu*. Each carrier contributed nine fighters for escort. Nagumo could not know that there was no chance his attack would gain surprise over the island. Captain Simard was taking no chances. He launched a dawn CAP at 0350hrs and followed this at 0415hrs with the launch of 22 PBYs for search operations. The 15 B-17s on the island were launched next to attack the Transport Group but with orders to head north if the Japanese carriers were located. The rest of Midway's strike aircraft were fueled and armed and waiting for a contact report to launch.

To meet the Japanese, the Marines at Midway scrambled every available fighter from Marine fighter squadron VMF-211. Six Wildcats and 18 F2A

Buffalos intercepted the Japanese 30 miles from Midway. The ensuing air battle, begun at 0620hrs, resulted in a disaster for the brave Marines. For a loss of 13 Buffalos and two Wildcats, Japanese losses were only one or two Zero fighters and three carrier attack planes. Most of the remaining Marine fighters were damaged; only two returned to Midway undamaged.

After brushing the Marines aside, the Japanese formation went on to strike targets on Eastern and Sand Islands, focusing on support facilities that were heavily damaged. No American aircraft was caught on the ground, and the defending antiaircraft fire was extremely heavy. Following the bombardment of Midway, the leader of the Japanese strike, *Hiryu*'s Lieutenant Tomonaga, signaled to Nagumo "there is need for a second attack wave." Not only had the strike failed to meet its objectives, but the cost to the Japanese was very high. Between the defending fighters and antiaircraft fire, 11 Japanese aircraft were shot down or ditched en route back to their carriers, including eight carrier attack planes, two fighters, and a single carrier bomber. Additionally, another 14 aircraft were heavily damaged and rendered nonoperational. Another 29 aircraft were damaged. Losses were particularly heavy in *Hiryu*'s carrier attack plane squadron. After the strike, only eight aircraft remained fully operational, which would prove to be important later in the day.

THE CARRIER BATTLE OF JUNE 4

Throughout the day, there was a calm breeze. This forced both sides to steam into the wind (to the southeast) at high speed to get sufficient wind over the deck to launch aircraft. This meant that the American carriers had to conduct flight operations by steaming away from the Japanese, thus increasing the distance their strike aircraft were required to fly to their targets. On the other hand, the Japanese had the potential advantage of generally steaming toward their targets while conducting flight operations.

At 0430hrs, the American carriers were some 200 miles north-northeast of Midway. As a precaution, Fletcher launched ten scout dive-bombers from *Yorktown* to perform reconnaissance to his north out to 100 miles. Fletcher's major advantage during the day was that he could rely on Midway to conduct the bulk of his reconnaissance. After launching his scouts, Fletcher headed to the northeast.

Few aspects of the battle have been as scrutinized as the Japanese reconnaissance program on the morning of June 4. Despite Nagumo's assumption that no American carriers were present, on the morning of June 4 Fletcher was located some 215 miles east of Nagumo, well within range of the Japanese scouts. All of the American advantages of superior intelligence would add up to nothing if the Japanese were successful in finding the Americans first.

To conduct his scouting, Nagumo devoted a total of seven aircraft. Six were ordered to fly to a range of 300 miles and the last out to 150 miles. At best, the Japanese reconnaissance efforts were half-hearted; at worst, they were negligent. Even in the words of Genda after the war, "the planning of the air searching was slipshod." With only seven aircraft, there were large gaps in the coverage even in good weather, and the weather was far from good, especially to the north, northeast, and the east. The lackluster search efforts simply reflected the Japanese belief that no American units would be present in the area. To top off Nagumo's potentially perilous situation, several of the search aircraft were not able to meet the scheduled 0430hrs launch time. The two aircraft from cruiser *Tone* were 12 and 30 minutes late getting off. Thus the already porous search plan was even more hazarded by the late start.

Unlike Nagumo's reconnaissance efforts, the Americans devoted considerable assets to reconnaissance. Both the Americans and Japanese believed that victory in a carrier battle was decided by which side could attack first, thus making good reconnaissance essential. The greater American emphasis on this aspect of the operation paid early dividends on June 4. At 0530hrs, the electrifying report "Enemy Carriers" was received by Fletcher from PBYs flying from Midway. This was followed at 0552hrs by a report from another PBY of "Many planes headed Midway, bearing 310 distance 150."

The initial vague report of enemy carriers had been amplified by the PBY, but this was not received aboard the American carriers. Midway rebroadcast the report to the aloft B-17s which was copied by Fletcher at 0603hrs: "Two carriers and battleships, bearing 320 degrees, distance 180, course 135, speed 25." Once plotted out by Fletcher's staff, the Japanese force was 247 degrees at 180 miles from TF-16. This was just within the strike range of the American air groups; however, the report was in error. The Japanese carriers sighted were actually 200 miles from TF-16, thus placing them slightly out of range of a full strike. The Japanese carriers were 220 miles from TF-17. Moreover, the report of only two carriers corresponded with the intelligence provided by Nimitz and created the concern in Fletcher's mind that the other two Japanese carriers remained unlocated.

LEFT
Yorktown pictured on the morning of June 4. Her air group is spotted on deck but has yet to begin launch. (US Naval Historical Center)

RIGHT
Heavy cruiser *Chikuma* showing the forward placement of all four of her 8in. gun turrets. The float planes carried aboard this ship and her sister *Tone* played an important part in Japanese search doctrine. Preferring to retain as many carrier strike aircraft as possible for offensive missions, the burden of search operations were placed on float planes from cruisers and battleships. (Yamato Museum)

TOP

Tone in 1942. The three larger aircraft aft are E13A1 Type 0 float reconnaissance aircraft and the smaller biplane is an E8N2 Type 95 float reconnaissance aircraft. At Midway, both *Tone* and *Chikuma* carried three Type 0 and two Type 95 aircraft. (*Ships of the World Magazine*)

BOTTOM

Torpedo Squadron 6 spotted on *Enterprise's* flight deck before being launched on the morning of June 4. Only four of these aircraft returned to *Enterprise*. (US Naval Historical Center)

After quick deliberation, Fletcher ordered Spruance at 0607hrs to head south and strike the reported contact. Fletcher would follow after *Yorktown* recovered her scout aircraft launched earlier that morning. Spruance and his chief of staff decided on a 0700hrs launch. It was calculated that by that time the Japanese would be some 155 miles from TF-16, within range of the short-legged American fighters and torpedo bombers. At 0638hrs, Spruance's flagship signaled to *Hornet* by blinking light to launch at 0700hrs. At this point, Mitscher and Ring and the various squadron commanders of *Hornet's* Air Group made a fateful decision. For reasons never fully explained, they decided to send the *Hornet's* strike group on a course of 265 degrees to the target, well to the north of the contact report. The report of only two carriers weighed heavily with Fletcher. The other two Japanese carriers thought to be in Nagumo's force could be operating in another group, perhaps far from the reported contact. Until the situation was clarified, Fletcher decided to hold *Yorktown's* aircraft in reserve. Around 0630hrs, *Yorktown* completed recovery of her ten scout aircraft and Fletcher headed to the southwest at high speed to follow Spruance.

The launch of TF-16's strike began as ordered at 0700hrs. *Hornet's* strike was in the air by 0742hrs, and at 0755hrs the strike departed. The fighters flew overhead at 21,000–22,000ft, just above the dive-bombers at 19,000ft with the torpedo aircraft at 1,500ft. On *Enterprise*, the launch did not go as smoothly. By 0745hrs, the second deckload was still not off, so Spruance ordered McClusky and the dive-bombers to proceed to the target. When finally airborne, *Enterprise's* fighters sighted and escorted *Hornet's* torpedo bomber squadron. Spruance had committed a total of 116 aircraft to the attack – 20 fighters, 67 dive-bombers, and 29 torpedo planes. However, the cohesion of the strike was already in question. Instead of two air groups heading to their targets in loose company ready to launch coordinated strikes, the American strike aircraft now proceeded in three groups. The largest was *Hornet*'s air group with VF-6 from *Enterprise* trailing behind. The delayed launch from *Enterprise* meant that her dive-bombers and torpedo aircraft proceeded in two separate groups. More importantly, each of the three groups was taking a separate course to the target.

MIDWAY ATTACKS THE 1ST KIDO BUTAI

As soon as Captain Simard on Midway received the contact report of Japanese carriers, he immediately launched all his operational strike aircraft. All of Midway's fighters were retained to defend the base, so the 51 strike aircraft from the US Navy, Marine Corps, and the Air Corps proceeded without escort.

Just after 0700hrs, the first American strike aircraft arrived in the area of Nagumo's force. Lookouts on *Akagi* spotted the first American aircraft. Over the 1st Kido Butai were 29 Zero fighters on CAP. The first wave of attackers consisted of six TBF Avenger torpedo planes, making their combat debut, and four US Army Air Corps B-26 Marauder medium bombers operating as torpedo bombers. Without escort, they were easy prey for the swarming Japanese fighters. Two TBFs were able to launch torpedoes on *Hiryu* and a single B-26 launched its weapon against *Akagi*, but all missed. Of the attacking aircraft, only a single Avenger and two Marauders survived to return to Midway. In return, two defending fighters were shot down.

Shortly after 0800hrs, the 16 Dauntless dive-bombers of Marine Squadron VMSB-241 arrived. The squadron's commander, Major Lofton Henderson, did not believe his inexperienced pilots could deliver a full dive-bomb attack, so he opted for a less steep and less demanding glide-bomb attack from 9,500ft on the nearest carrier in sight. With *Hiryu* as the target, the Marines began their attack against 13 Zero fighters on CAP, quickly joined by another six. No hits were scored; eight Marine aircraft were shot down, including Major Henderson's, at the cost of a single *Hiryu* fighter.

A view of the sole surviving TBF Avenger to return to Midway after the six aircraft from VT-8's Midway detachment conducted a morning attack on the 1st Kido Butai on June 4. The aircraft never flew again. (US Naval Historical Center)

The next American aircraft to attack were 14 B-17s, which delivered a high-altitude attack on *Soryu*, *Hiryu* and *Akagi* from an altitude of over 20,000ft. Nine fighters from *Soryu* and three from *Kaga* engaged the heavy bombers, but no aircraft were lost on either side. By 0820hrs, the B-17 attack was completed with no hits scored.

Midway's final attack was conducted by 11 SB2U-3 dive-bombers from VMSB-241. These were obsolescent aircraft making their only combat appearance during the war. Unwilling to attempt to penetrate the wall of fighters to reach the carriers, they delivered a glide-bomb attack on battleship *Haruna*. Three aircraft were lost for no hits.

NAGUMO'S DILEMMA

After his Midway strike departed, Nagumo still held a large reserve force in readiness. As per Yamamoto's orders to Nagumo delivered during war games held in May, Nagumo was to maintain half his strike aircraft armed for attacks on naval units to counter any American ships making an appearance. Aboard *Akagi* and *Kaga*, 43 carrier attack planes stood ready armed with torpedoes with 34 carrier bombers on *Hiryu* and *Soryu* (these were not yet armed – this was done on the flight deck after the aircraft were spotted for launch).

Following the recommendation from Tomonaga at 0715hrs advising that a second Midway strike was required, Nagumo decided to disobey Yamamoto's orders to keep half his strike aircraft armed for ship attack and ordered that his reserve aircraft be prepared for land attack in order to launch the second attack on Midway. This required that the carrier attack planes have their torpedoes exchanged for 800kg bombs and that the carrier bombers be loaded with high-explosive bombs, unsuited for attacking ships. In Nagumo's mind, this was justified since the search planes were scheduled to have reached their furthest points and had yet to report anything.

Just as this re-arming process was beginning, Nagumo received very disturbing news. At 0740hrs, *Tone*'s search plane Number 4 flying the 100 degrees search route from base reported contact with an American task force: "Sight what appears to be ten enemy surface ships, in position bearing 010 degrees distance 250 miles from Midway. Course 150 degrees, speed over 20 knots." Though frustratingly vague on the types of ships, this contact report was actually a stroke of luck for Nagumo. *Tone*'s Number 4 aircraft had been 30 minutes late in launching, but for some reason had cut its route short and flew its scheduled dog-leg to the north early. This placed the floatplane in a position to make its contact report. The aircraft that should have contacted the American force was cruiser *Chikuma*'s Number 1 search plane flying the 77 degrees route. Had this aircraft been flying its correct route and had it been at its correct altitude to spot ships in the scattered clouds, it would have passed within some 20 miles of the American carriers. Owing to poor navigation or cloud cover, or both, it never reported contact.

Though this initial report made no mention of carriers, it obviously meant the US Navy was present in strength. At 0745hrs, Nagumo ordered the suspension of the re-arming process of his reserve aircraft. He instructed the *Tone* aircraft to "Ascertain ship types and maintain contact." Finally, at 0830hrs, *Tone* Number 4 filled out its incomplete earlier report delivering the alarming report "the enemy is accompanied by what appears to be a carrier."

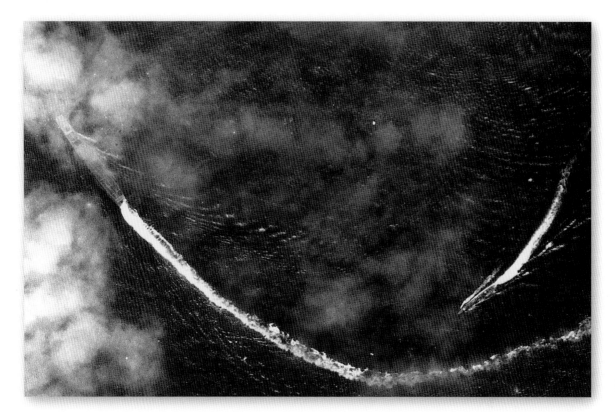

Nagumo still retained a large strike force of 43 torpedo aircraft partially re-armed with bombs and 34 dive-bombers partially armed with high-explosive bombs. Nagumo's real problem was that he believed only six Zero fighters intended for strike escort were still available. The rest had been launched to fend off Midway's attacks. Compounding Nagumo's difficulties was the arrival overhead of his Midway strike with many aircraft low on fuel or damaged. Predictably, the aggressive Yamaguchi advised Nagumo to launch an immediate strike against the American carrier, even if it was not properly escorted.

Akagi pictured under attack by B-17s during the 0800hrs engagement on June 4. The ship trailing *Akagi* is the Kagero-class destroyer *Nowaki*, assigned as *Akagi*'s plane guard. No aircraft are evident on *Akagi*'s flight deck. Easily seen is the large Rising Sun painted on the forward part of the flight deck. (US Naval Historical Center)

At this juncture, Nagumo was truly on the horns of a dilemma. His basic assumption that the Americans would not be present until after Midway was captured was shown to be incorrect. His search plan had proven inadequate, but at least the Americans had been located. Midway remained a threat, and, increasing the need for an immediate decision, Nagumo's Midway strike aircraft were due to return to the 1st Kido Butai by 0815hrs. Now, the decision to disobey Yamamoto's orders to retain a reserve for ship attack meant that his reserve force was not ready to attack the American task force. With perfect hindsight, it should have been obvious what the first *Tone* contact report meant, even without an identification of ship types. What were 10 ships doing 240 miles north-northeast of Midway (on Nagumo's flank) heading 150 degrees (into the wind)? Had Nagumo launched his strike force immediately, almost all of the aircraft would have still been armed for ship attack and the force could have been spotted and launched before the Midway strike aircraft had to land. Enough fighters could have been found to provide a sufficient escort. However, since no immediate action was taken, the initiative again passed to the Americans. At 0753hrs, battleship *Kirishima* spotted another group of approaching American aircraft. For the next 40

49

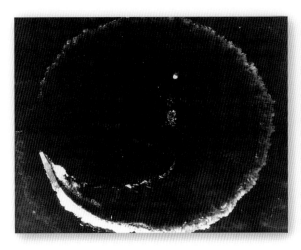

minutes, the 1st Kido Butai was attacked by three more groups of American aircraft. Because the decks of all four carriers were busy handling CAP launches and recoveries, this meant that there was no chance to bring the reserve aircraft up from the hangar decks and spot them for launch.

After weighing all his options, Nagumo decided to take the cautious course. He would recover his Midway strike, and then proceed to the northeast to close the American contact while preparing a 1030hrs strike. This would include 34 carrier bombers, 43 carrier attack planes armed with torpedoes, and 12 fighter escorts. Until the strike could be launched, the CAP could provide defense against the brave but ineffective American attacks. At 0837hrs, the 1st Kido Butai turned into the wind to recover aircraft. At 0918hrs, the recovery complete, Nagumo changed course to the northeast and increased speed to 30 knots to close the American force. If he could only get the time to prepare for his planned 1030hrs launch, his veteran aviators would make short work of the American carrier. In reality, whatever course Nagumo decided upon, it was probably already too late. The American carrier aircraft launched at 0700hrs were already well on their way to the Japanese carriers.

FLETCHER'S SITUATION

At 0815hrs, the radar aboard *Enterprise* detected an unidentified aircraft to the south approximately 30 miles away. Though CAP aircraft were vectored to intercept, no contact was made with the intruder. This was *Tone* plane Number 4 which soon reported contact with Fletcher's carriers. Since the Americans intercepted the contact report, Fletcher knew his carriers had been sighted. He was still worried that the morning contact report mentioned only two Japanese carriers and that the two unreported carriers might be preparing a strike. He had waited further into the morning for the situation to be clarified and had accordingly delayed launching *Yorktown's* strike. Now, assuming he had been spotted and not wanting to be caught with fueled and armed planes on deck, Fletcher decided to launch part of *Yorktown's* strike. Between 0830 and 0905hrs, 17 dive-bombers from VB-3, 12 torpedo bombers from VT-3, and six fighter escorts were launched. The entire strike headed off on a course of 240 degrees from TF-17. Fletcher still retained a strike force of 17 dive-bombers from VS-5 together with six fighters.

The carrier battle of June 4: flight tracks of the American air groups

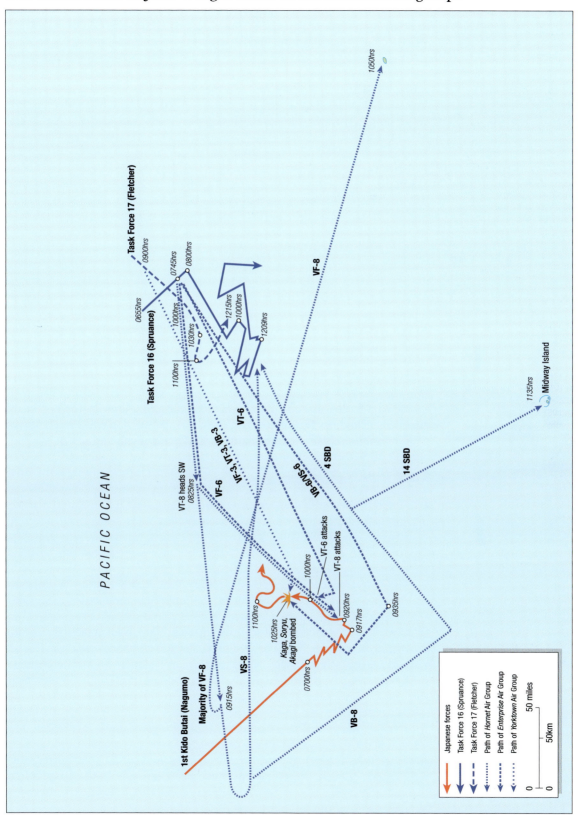

PACIFIC OCEAN

Task Force 17 (Fletcher)
Task Force 16 (Spruance)
1st Kido Butai (Nagumo)
Majority of VF-8
Midway Island

0900hrs
0745hrs
0800hrs
0655hrs
1000hrs
1030hrs
1215hrs
1000hrs
1209hrs
1100hrs
1050hrs
1135hrs

VF-8
VT-6
VF-6
VT-3, VT-3, VB-3
VB-6/VS-6
4 SBD
14 SBD

VT-8 heads SW
0825hrs

VS-8
VB-8

0915hrs
0700hrs
1100hrs
1025hrs
0917hrs
0920hrs
0935hrs

1000hrs
VT-6 attacks
VT-8 attacks

Kaga, Soryu, Akagi bombed

Legend

Japanese forces
Task Force 16 (Spruance)
Task Force 17 (Fletcher)
Path of *Hornet* Air Group
Path of *Enterprise* Air Group
Path of *Yorktown* Air Group

0   50 miles
0   50km

THE DECISIVE PHASE

Aircraft from three US carriers were now winging toward Nagumo's carriers. Aside from a single squadron remaining on *Yorktown*, this amounted to every strike aircraft that Fletcher could put in the air. Up until this point, the CAP over the 1st Kido Butai had done a superb job defending the carriers. However, the assailants they had faced so far were a makeshift force not well trained in attacking ships. If the American carrier aircraft could find their targets, Japanese air defense capabilities would be tested like never before.

What ensued for the next hour and a half, from 0915hrs until the last American torpedo bombers departed at 1040hrs, decided the battle. During that time, the 1st Kido Butai would go from a seemingly invincible to a defeated force. The American inability to orchestrate coordinated strikes was on full display, as was the bravery and skill of the US pilots. Despite the lack of cohesion, the fortunes of war placed the US Navy's most accurate and powerful weapons over three undefended Japanese carriers at the exact moment when they were most vulnerable.

The first to attack was *Hornet*'s torpedo plane squadron. Lieutenant Commander John Waldron took his 15 Devastator aircraft on the course of 265 degrees, as briefed, flying at 1,500ft. At 0825hrs, he broke away from Ring's formation and took his squadron to the southwest where he was certain the enemy would be. He was exactly right. Waldron spotted smoke and then the Japanese carriers at 0915hrs. *Chikuma* sighted the approaching torpedo planes to the northeast at approximately 20 miles. Commencing an immediate attack, Waldron's squadron went to wave-top level and began an attack run at the 1st Kido Butai which was heading directly toward them. Waldron picked out the nearest carrier to him, which happened to be *Soryu*. The Japanese had 18 fighters aloft on CAP, and, as the attack developed, *Akagi* and *Kaga* launched another 11. The only form of defense possessed by the Devastators was to fly as low as possible. This did not stop the slow aircraft from being hacked down mercilessly by the swarming Zeros. Between 0920 and 0937hrs, all 15 Devastators were destroyed but not until a single aircraft launched its torpedo at 800 yards against *Soryu*'s starboard side with no success. The sacrifice of VT-8 was important, not because it drew the Japanese CAP down to low altitudes but because it prevented the Japanese from beginning to spot their strike aircraft.

The next American aircraft to make an appearance were the 14 Devastators of VT-6 from *Enterprise*. After launch, the squadron commander, Lieutenant Commander Eugene Lindsey, flew his briefed course of 240 degrees and after 0930hrs sighted smoke 30 miles to the northwest. He soon converted this into a visual of the 1st Kido Butai headed to the northeast at high speed. He decided to head for the nearest carrier, *Kaga*, and conduct a split attack. The Japanese CAP was now up to 27 fighters and lookouts had spotted the approaching torpedo planes from the south at 0938hrs. At 0940hrs, *Tone* opened fire with her main battery to mark the location of the attackers for the CAP. Meanwhile, *Akagi* and *Soryu* launched another seven fighters at 0945hrs. The 14 Devastators began their attack runs under heavy fire, and this time at least five were able to launch against *Kaga*, but the extreme range and bad angles of the torpedo launch prevented any hits. The surviving Devastators exited through the center of the 1st Kido Butai to the east. Of the five surviving aircraft, one later ditched before reaching *Enterprise*.

Enterprise maneuvering at high speed during the battle of Midway with an escorting cruiser in the background. Midway marked the finest moment of the US Navy's most decorated ship. The ship's air group destroyed two Japanese carriers and joined in the destruction of a third. (US Naval Historical Center)

Circling overhead at 22,000ft during the slaughter of the American torpedo bombers were the 10 Wildcats of Lieutenant Gray's VF-6. By 0950hrs, he had been overhead the 1st Kido Butai for 30 minutes, undiscovered by the Japanese the entire time. He had not heard the pleas of VT-6 for help as they commenced their attack, so, after making a contact report at 0956hrs, Gray returned to *Enterprise* minutes later. Only as he prepared to depart the area were his aircraft spotted by the Japanese.

The fate of *Hornet*'s strike is one of the most controversial aspects of the battle. Despite the fact that the Japanese lay on a course of 240 degrees from TF-16 when the PBY contact report was received, *Hornet*'s Air Group was ordered to fly a course of 265 degrees to the target. Torpedo Squadron 8 departed on the 265 degrees heading but altered course to the southwest at about 0825hrs and had no problem finding the Japanese with the results already discussed. Commander Ring and his 34 Dauntlesses from VB-8 and VS-8, escorted by 10 VF-8 fighters, flew a course of 265 degrees at 19,000ft and passed well north of 1st Kido Butai. Between 150–160 miles out, VF-8 departed from Ring and returned to *Hornet* becasue of lack of fuel. All VF-8 aircraft were unable to find *Hornet* and all ten were forced to ditch. Eventually all but two of the pilots were rescued. At 225 miles out, the formation totally disintegrated, with Ring and 14 aircraft of VS-8 headed east to *Hornet*, again passing to the north of 1st Kido Butai. The remaining 18 VB-8 aircraft continued south in an attempt to locate the Japanese carriers. When they finally turned east, they were now south of the 1st Kido Butai. Four of the aircraft continued to the northeast to recover on *Hornet*, but the rest of the group turned to the southeast to land on Midway. The largest single component of TF-16's strike had not even seen the enemy.

Fortunately for the Americans, the fate of *Enterprise*'s dive-bombers was very different. The 33 aircraft of VB-6 and VS-6 (reduced to 32 after the abort of a VS-6 Dauntless) under McClusky departed on a course of 231 degrees and planned to find the Japanese at about 140 miles out. Upon reaching this point, and seeing no sign of the Japanese, McClusky figured he was south of the Japanese and decided to head to the northwest at 0935hrs. At 1000hrs, he planned to take a northeasterly course. Almost at the end of his planned northwesterly track, at 0955hrs he spotted a Japanese destroyer steaming north-northeasterly at high speed. McClusky made the logical assessment that the destroyer was hurrying to rejoin Nagumo's force. He was correct – the ship below was the destroyer *Arashi* heading toward Nagumo after depth-charging the American submarine *Nautilus*. At 1002hrs, McClusky reported sighting Nagumo 35 miles to the northeast.

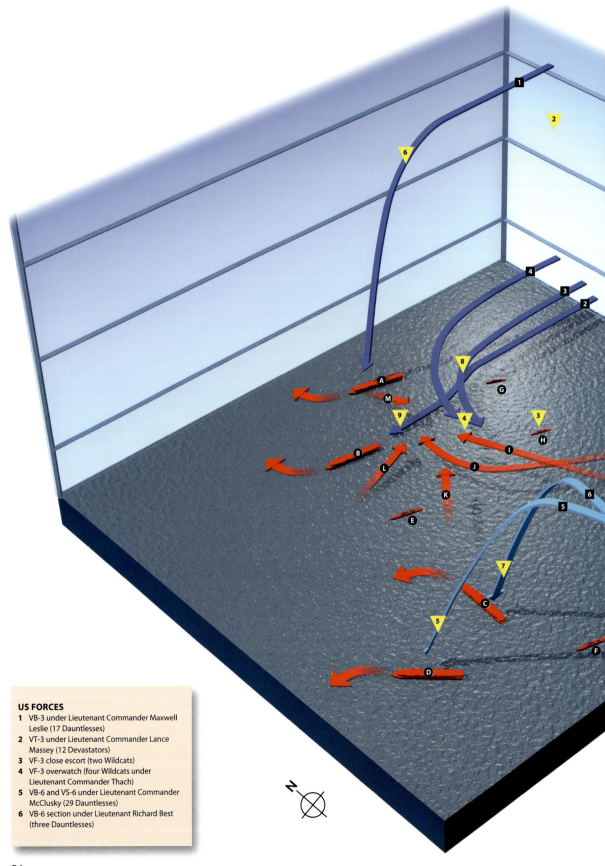

US FORCES
1 VB-3 under Lieutenant Commander Maxwell
  Leslie (17 Dauntlesses)
2 VT-3 under Lieutenant Commander Lance
  Massey (12 Devastators)
3 VF-3 close escort (two Wildcats)
4 VF-3 overwatch (four Wildcats under
  Lieutenant Commander Thach)
5 VB-6 and VS-6 under Lieutenant Commander
  McClusky (29 Dauntlesses)
6 VB-6 section under Lieutenant Richard Best
  (three Dauntlesses)

15,000ft

10,000ft

5,000ft

10

1

JAPANESE FORCES

A *Soryu*
B *Hiryu*
C *Akagi*
D *Kaga*
E *Haruna*
F *Kirishima*
G *Tone*
H *Chikuma*
I CAP over carriers (14 Zeros)
J CAP chasing remnants of VT-6 southeast of carriers (11 Zeros)
K CAP to southeast of carriers (ten Zeros)
L CAP launching from *Hiryu* (three Zeros)
M CAP launching from *Soryu* (three Zeros)

▼ **EVENTS**

1 1002hrs: McClusky spots 1st Kido Butai 35 miles to northeast.

2 1003hrs: *Yorktown* strike spots 1st Kido Butai to northwest.

3 1010hrs: *Chikuma* spots VT-3 14 miles from Japanese carriers. 35 Zeros are on CAP with six more preparing to launch. All airborne CAP is at low altitude.

4 1010–1030hrs: dogfight between VF-3 and Japanese CAP. The six Wildcats from VF-3 and the torpedo aircraft from VT-3 are attacked by the majority of the Japanese CAP, though exact numbers are unknown. During this confused action, one Wildcat and up to six Zeros are shot down, three by Thach. Only one Devastator is lost.

5 1022hrs: McClusky and his command section, VS-6 and most of VB-6 attack *Kaga*. Against minimal antiaircraft fire and no CAP, four hits are scored, dooming the carrier.

6 1025hrs: VB-3 with 17 aircraft, of which only 13 carry bombs, attack *Soryu*. Against light antiaircraft fire and no CAP, three hits are scored, setting the ship on fire.

7 1026hrs: Best breaks off from attack on *Kaga* with two other VB-6 aircraft and moves north to attack *Akagi*. Despite watching the devastation on *Kaga*, *Akagi* is surprised. Best puts a 1,000-pound bomb on the ship's middle elevator which penetrates to the hangar deck and starts a large fire which cannot be contained.

8 1030hrs: after reaching torpedo range, Massey decides not to launch torpedoes owing to a poor attack angle. He continues to the north, parallel to the 1st Kido Butai, to gain a better position. This gives the Japanese CAP more opportunity to attack.

9 1035–1040hrs: VT-3 reaches attack position and drops five torpedoes against *Hiryu*'s starboard side from between 600 and 800 yards. No hits are scored.

10 1045hrs: US strike aircraft complete withdrawal under attack by Zeros. Of VT-3's 12 aircraft, only two survive. None of VB-3's aircraft are attacked by CAP and all 17 return. About one-third of *Enterprise*'s dive-bombers are attacked by CAP departing the area of the 1st Kido Butai, but combat losses total only two aircraft from either CAP or antiaircraft fire. However, only 15 of 33 Dauntlesses return to *Enterprise*.

THE BATTLE IS DECIDED
US aircraft attack and fatally damage three Japanese carriers on the morning of June 4.

Soryu in 1939. For her size, *Soryu* possessed a large offensive punch. (Yamato Museum)

As McClusky took an indirect route to his target, the strike from *Yorktown* took a direct route to the 1st Kido Butai. The performance of *Yorktown*'s Air Group was by far the best on June 4; generally missed in the chaotic American attacks that day on the 1st Kido Butai was that *Yorktown*'s dive-bomber and torpedo squadron launched a generally coordinated attack. By chance, this attack developed at the same time McClusky's aircraft arrived in the target area.

After launch, *Yorktown*'s three airborne squadrons rendezvoused at 0945hrs. VB-3 flew at 15,000ft, with the torpedo aircraft of VT-3 at 1,500ft protected by two groups of fighters above them. At 1003hrs, both VT-3 and VB-3 spotted the Japanese force to the northwest. VT-3 went to 2,600ft for a high-level approach which allowed the aircraft to pick up air speed in a dive during the approach.

At the time of the approach of *Yorktown*'s Air Group and of McClusky's dive-bombers, 41 Japanese Zero fighters were already aloft on CAP or just scrambling. Fourteen fighters were near the carriers, 11 were chasing the remnants of VT-6, and another ten were located out to the southeast. Another six, three each from *Hiryu* and *Soryu*, were preparing to launch. All of the fighters were at low altitude, the result of just having dealt with the attacks from *Hornet*'s and then *Enterprise*'s torpedo bomber squadrons.

At 1010hrs, *Chikuma* gave the initial warning of another impending attack. She spotted the Devastators of VT-3 when they were still 14 miles from the nearest carrier and fired her main battery in the direction of the oncoming aircraft to alert the CAP. The arrival of another fresh group of torpedo aircraft prompted the fighters chasing the departing VT-6 to break off and turn their attention to VT-3. However, unlike the previous torpedo plane attacks, VT-3 had the advantage of an escort by six Wildcats; two of these provided close escort at 3,000ft with another four under Thach maintaining watch from 5,500ft. A large number of Zero fighters were attracted to Thach's small formation. Up to 20 Japanese fighters launched continual attacks, shooting down one of Thach's Wildcats. The remaining three went into the defensive formation known as the Thach Weave and successfully warded off the Japanese fighters, shooting down three.

The two Wildcats on close escort for VT-3 successfully defended their charges, shooting down two Japanese fighters in the process. The result of the fighter duel between the six fighters of VF-3 and the 1st Kido Butai's CAP was that virtually all the defending fighters were drawn into the fight at low altitudes. Only a single VT-3 Devastator was shot down before the torpedo planes leveled off at 150ft for their final attack run.

To present their stern to the approaching VT-3 torpedo bombers, Nagumo decided to turn to the northwest. The squadron's commanding officer, Lieutenant Commander Lance Massey, decided to pass up this poor attack angle and head to the north to attack the last carrier in sight, *Hiryu*. This forced VT-3 to run parallel to the 1st Kido Butai, giving the Japanese CAP additional opportunities to attack.

As *Yorktown*'s torpedo bombers approached, no Japanese observer spotted the arrival of VB-3 at 15,000ft. Likewise, the arrival of McClusky's dive-bombers also went unnoticed. The 17 dive-bombers of VB-3 selected *Soryu* as their target. Of these, only 13 were still armed with bombs after a faulty electrical arming switch resulted in the loss of the 1,000-pound bombs aboard the squadron commander's aircraft and three others. Beginning at 1025hrs, VB-3 scored three hits on *Soryu*. No aircraft were lost to antiaircraft fire or CAP.

Of the 32 dive-bombers with McClusky, 30 dived on targets. By doctrine, each of the two squadrons present would take a single target. McClusky ordered the leading squadron, VS-6, to hit the nearest carrier, *Kaga*, and for VB-6 to hit the more distant *Akagi*. However, this was exactly contrary to existing doctrine, so, in the resulting confusion, both squadrons prepared to dive on *Kaga*. At 1022hrs, McClusky and his two wingmen, VS-6, and most of VB-6 commenced their dives on *Kaga*. With no CAP present and no antiaircraft fire, the result was devastating. Four bombs hit the ship, turning her almost instantly into an inferno.

As the *Soryu* and *Kaga* were dealt mortal damage, it appeared that *Akagi* would survive unscathed. However, in one of the most important moments of the battle, Lieutenant Richard Best, commanding officer of VB-6, realized that both *Enterprise* squadrons were attacking *Kaga* and that *Akagi* might go untouched. Best and two other VB-6 aircraft aborted their dives on *Kaga* and proceeded north to attack *Akagi*. Attacking from *Akagi*'s port side, they gained total surprise. One aircraft scored a near miss alongside *Akagi*'s stern, and Best placed a 1,000-pound bomb on the aft edge of the middle elevator. This then penetrated to the upper hangar where it exploded among the armed and fueled aircraft. The entire attack by *Enterprise*'s dive-bombers cost only two VB-6 aircraft, which were destroyed by either low-flying CAP on their withdrawal or by antiaircraft fire.

An SBD Dauntless ditches astern of heavy cruiser *Astoria* on June 4. In the distance is a PBY patrol plane and a destroyer. Dauntless losses were heavy on June 4. (US Naval Historical Center)

Between 1035 and 1040hrs, the last attack of the morning against the 1st Kido Butai was completed. After taking his Devastators to a better attack position, Massey attempted to get *Hiryu* in a split attack. Five Devastators launched against *Hiryu*'s starboard side between 600 and 800 yards, but none hit. Ten of the 12 Devastators were shot down.

With this, the American attack was over. A total of eight bombs had been placed on three carriers. *Hiryu* was untouched by dive-bombing and torpedo attack and remained undamaged. Compared with the fatal damage suffered by the three carriers, aircraft losses mattered little. However, losses on both sides had been heavy. Of the up to 41 Japanese fighters on CAP, 11 were shot down, and three more ditched. In return, they inflicted crippling losses on the early piecemeal American strikes, but were unable to defend the carriers from dive-bomber attack.

Enterprise's and *Hornet*'s returning aircraft had a difficult time finding TF-16 because their carriers were not in the location where they had been briefed. Throughout the day, Spruance's staff failed to perform basic staff functions adequately. *Hornet*'s Air Group suffered the most. VF-8 missed TF-16 entirely and all ten aircraft were lost. Most of the aircraft from VB-8 decided to head to Midway. Three ditched en route and three more were damaged by friendly antiaircraft fire during their approach. Commander Ring returned to *Hornet* with VS-8. *Hornet*'s Air Group had inflicted no damage on the enemy. In the process they had lost 15 torpedo planes, 10 fighters, and only 20 of 34 dive-bombers recovered aboard the carrier. *Enterprise*'s strike fared better, but losses were still heavy. Her dive-bombers had inflicted mortal damage on two carriers. All 10 VF-6 fighters returned, but only four torpedo bombers out of 14 returned, and of the 33 dive-bombers dispatched, only 15 returned.

Yorktown's VB-3 returned at 1115hrs, but was ordered to remain aloft in order not to break the deck spot. Eventually, with their carrier under attack, 15 VB-3 aircraft recovered aboard *Enterprise*. Still concerned about the possibility of undetected Japanese carriers, Fletcher decided to launch a search with 10 VS-5 aircraft to cover the northwest sector out to 200 miles. The last seven Dauntlesses were kept fueled and armed in reserve.

THE JAPANESE RESPONSE

In the aftermath of the American dive-bombing attack, the condition of all three damaged Japanese carriers was perilous. Unless prompt and effective damage-control measures could be taken to avoid the spread of fire, all three would be lost. Despite persistent myth, none of the three carriers had its strike aircraft spotted on the flight deck when it was attacked. However, these aircraft were below on the hangar decks, armed and fueled. Additionally, the hectic morning of arming aircraft and then re-arming them for a different mission left large amounts of ordnance around the hangars. In these conditions, even a single bomb hit could prove catastrophic.

Not surprisingly, the fate of the smaller *Soryu* was the first to be decided. The three hits at approximately 1025hrs set off huge fires which quickly spread to the second hangar deck. Soon, the fires covered the ship from stem to stern. At 1040hrs, the ship went dead in the water. By 1045hrs, it was obvious that the fight had been lost and Captain Yanagimoto ordered the ship to be abandoned. *Soryu* sank that evening at 1913hrs with the loss of 711 officers and men, including her captain who refused to leave his ship.

This photo shows *Hiryu* launching Type 99 carrier bombers. One has just taken off and a second is already circling to the ship's port side. This photo was taken during the Midway operation, and almost certainly shows the launch of Lieutenant Kobayashi's strike around 1100hrs on June 4. (Yamato Museum)

The bombs that struck *Kaga* penetrated to the upper hangar deck, igniting fires from the aircraft and ordnance there. One of the four bombs hit the bridge, killing, among others, Captain Okada and the ship's damage-control officer. This left the fight against the raging flames under the control of the ship's inexperienced senior aviators. The flames could not be controlled and soon all power was lost. At 1410hrs, the American submarine *Nautilus*, which had been playing a cat-and-mouse game all morning with various escorts of the 1st Kido Butai, attacked *Kaga*. Though one torpedo hit the carrier, it failed to explode. Having failed to bring the intense fires under control, all surviving crew members were taken off by destroyers and at 1925hrs, the ship was scuttled with destroyer torpedoes. Losses from her crew totaled 811 officers and men.

The death of *Akagi* was the most prolonged. Ordinarily, the single bomb hit at 1026hrs would not have been fatal, but the well-placed bomb had penetrated to the hangar deck where it ignited the fueled and armed carrier attack planes located there. The crew was unable to localize the flames to a single portion of the hangar deck, and they soon spread to the flight deck. At 1042hrs, the ship's steering failed, probably because of the near-miss astern. Nagumo could not command the 1st Kido Butai from a burning carrier with a jammed rudder, so at 1046hrs he left the ship after evacuating the bridge by means of a rope through the bridge windows to avoid the fires. Despite the best efforts of Captain Aoki and the damage-control personnel, the ship lost power at 1350hrs which crippled the crew's ability to fight the raging fires. "Abandon ship" was ordered approximately at 1700hrs. After much anguish, Yamamoto personally ordered the ship scuttled the next morning. Only 263 of her crew were lost.

The morning's disaster left only a single carrier operational – *Hiryu*. With Nagumo unable to exercise effective command from the burning *Akagi*, temporary command of the 1st Kido Butai fell to Rear Admiral Abe Hiroaki, commander of Cruiser Division 8. He detached the light cruiser *Nagara* and six destroyers to stand by the three burning carriers and formed the remainder of the escort ships, two battleships, two heavy cruisers, and five destroyers around *Hiryu*.

On board *Hiryu*, Yamaguchi received orders from Abe to launch an immediate strike on the American carriers. Yamaguchi decided to commit *Hiryu*'s carrier bomber unit and to follow this up with a strike by *Hiryu*'s remaining carrier attack aircraft one hour later. Both would be given an escort of six fighters. *Hiryu*'s remaining air strength was not great: only 36 fully operational aircraft were on board – 10 fighters, 18 dive-bombers and eight torpedo planes. These would be reinforced by the 27 CAP fighters still aloft, but Yamaguchi would have to be careful about employing his sparse strike assets.

Lieutenant Kobayashi Michio was the commander of *Hiryu's* Carrier Bomber Unit which showed considerable skill and determination during the strike against *Yorktown* on the afternoon of June 4. (US Naval Historical Center)

Much was expected of *Hiryu's* first strike, led by Lieutenant Kobayashi Michio, commander of *Hiryu's* carrier bombers. The 18 carrier bombers were all piloted by veterans and were considered an elite unit. They would have ample chance to prove it. After a brief by *Hiryu's* captain, the 24 aircraft were launched at 1050hrs, and by 1058hrs the group headed to the west. At this point, the American carriers were less than 100 miles away.

While the Japanese had decided on an immediate strike from *Hiryu*, they remained unclear on the composition of the American force they were facing. Clear thinking on the part of the Japanese would have indicated that the size of the air attacks that had just devastated the 1st Kido Butai could have come only from several carriers. Much of the confusion was attributable to the incomplete reports of *Tone* aircraft Number 4. At 0855hrs, *Chikuma* aircraft Number 5 was dispatched to amplify the earlier contact reports on TF-16. Joining the aircraft from *Tone* and *Chikuma* was another scout plane from *Soryu*, the experimental D4Y1 Type 2 carrier bomber acting as a high-speed reconnaissance aircraft. After 1100hrs, it also arrived in the area of the American carriers and was able to confirm that three were present, though a faulty radio prevented this information from reaching Yamaguchi immediately. Around 1300hrs, the commander of Destroyer Division 4 reported the results of the interrogation of a captured VT-3 pilot (later murdered by the crew of the destroyer *Arashi*). The captured pilot confirmed the identification of the three US carriers and indicated that *Yorktown* was operating separately. The information was confirmed by *Soryu's* D4Y1 when it returned to land on *Hiryu* at about 1300hrs.

After evacuating *Akagi*, Nagumo transferred to the light cruiser *Nagara*. By early afternoon, he had caught up with the main body of the 1st Kido Butai and had resumed command. Determined to avenge the events of the morning, Nagumo ordered what remained of the 1st Kido Butai to head toward the Americans, now believed to be only 90 miles away. *Hiryu* would launch air strikes followed by what Nagumo optimistically believed would be an immediate surface engagement in which the Japanese heavy units would smash the Americans. The fanciful notion that the Americans would oblige Nagumo's desire for a surface engagement was shattered when at 1240hrs *Chikuma* aircraft Number 5 provided Nagumo with an update. The American force was opening the distance from the 1st Kido Butai and was headed north. In response to this information, and the realization that his surface ships stood little chance of catching the American carriers, Nagumo changed course to due north. Spruance was having nothing of the notion that the American carriers would be caught by Japanese surface units.

The first indication beyond the 1st Kido Butai that things were not going to plan was a 1050hrs message from Abe that *Akagi*, *Kaga* and *Soryu* were on fire and that only *Hiryu* remained operational. The shock felt by Yamamoto after receiving this news can be only imagined. After considering his options, he issued a flood of orders in an attempt to retrieve the situation. At 1220hrs, he directed the Main Body south to assist Nagumo. While the transports of the Invasion Force moved to the northwest to await developments, Kondo's combat units were ordered to the east to join Nagumo. The 2nd Kido Butai supporting the Aleutians operations was ordered to move south. At 1310hrs, he instructed Kondo to "shell and destroy" the airfield on Midway. With Midway eliminated, only the American carriers remained as a threat. These could be dealt with by strikes from *Hiryu* and an overwhelming surface attack.

HIRYU RETALIATES

With the American carriers only some 90 miles away and with the help of the Japanese aircraft now shadowing them, Kobayashi had no difficulty finding his target. En route to the American carriers, at about 1130hrs, the Japanese strike spotted six US aircraft. Impulsively, the aggressive fighter escort peeled off to engage. In the ensuing melee, two of the escorting Japanese fighters were damaged and were forced to return. Now the already inadequate strike escort was reduced to a mere four fighters.

The first indication by the Americans that the Japanese response was in progress was received at 1151hrs when *Yorktown*'s radar gained contact on an inbound group of unidentified aircraft to the southwest 32 miles from the ship. This development came at a bad time for the Americans. Twelve Wildcats had just been hurriedly launched at 1150hrs to clear the deck as a relief for the CAP and the six fighters concluding their CAP rotation were landing. Subsequently, the just-launched CAP was not well deployed and was not at its proper altitude.

At 1155hrs, the Japanese strike formation sighted TF-17 some 25 miles away. Kobayashi took his 18 carrier bombers into a climb to gain attack altitude. The four escort Zeros were miles behind as a result of the poor decision to attack the group of American stragglers, and were still trying to catch up. They did, however, spot the American fighters desperately attempting to gain altitude to intercept the Japanese bombers.

When the American fighters reached 10,000ft, the 18 Japanese carrier bombers were in two groups of nine, one slightly above the other. An immediate slashing attack by five Wildcats on one group and then a head-on attack on the second completely shattered the Japanese formation. Seven carrier bombers were dispatched, three by a single Wildcat. The second phase of the air engagement was more confused and included the late intervention of the Japanese fighter escort. Eight carrier bombers with bombs and two without survived the interception. The armed aircraft broke into two groups. One group of three headed east toward *Yorktown* and another group of five circled to the southwest to approach from out of the sun. These five aircraft survived two potentially devastating intercepts while losing only a single carrier bomber before attacking *Yorktown*.

Yorktown's escort of two cruisers and five destroyers was arranged in a circle 1,500–2,000 yards from the carrier. The entire group changed course to the southeast to head away from the Japanese aircraft. At 1209hrs, *Yorktown* sighted the Japanese aircraft closing from astern and from the starboard quarter. The experienced Japanese lined up to dive out of the sun and dispersed to attack from different bearings to confuse *Yorktown*'s gunners.

Yorktown under dive-bombing attack. One Type 99 carrier bomber is about to splash, minus its tail, forward of *Yorktown*. Another carrier bomber is visible above *Yorktown* after completing its dive. Its bomb can be seen to explode aft of the carrier. This was probably the attack of Petty Officer Tsuchiya, who flew the third aircraft to dive on *Yorktown*. (US Naval Historical Center)

Duel of the carriers: tracks of the opposing forces on June 4

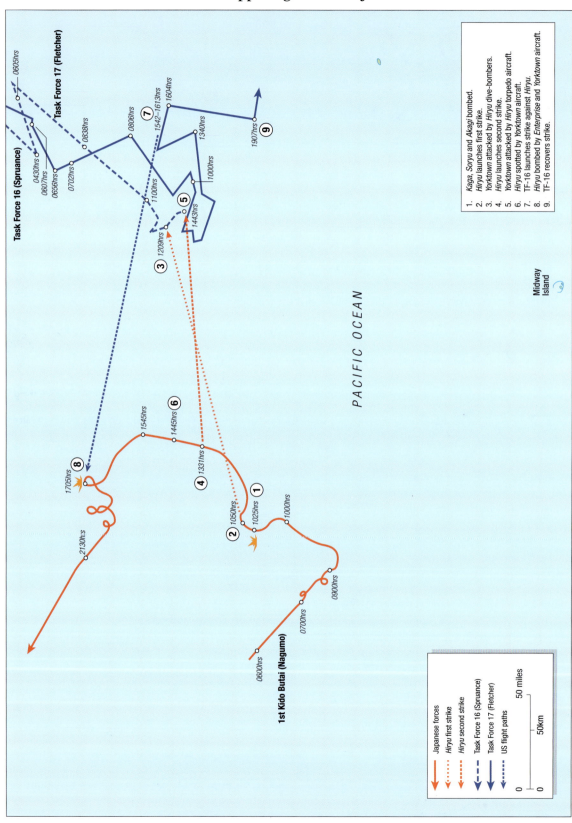

1st Kido Butai (Nagumo)

Task Force 16 (Spruance)

Task Force 17 (Fletcher)

0605hrs
0430hrs
0607hrs
0656hrs
0702hrs
0838hrs
0806hrs
1542–1613hrs
1604hrs
1340hrs
1100hrs
1209hrs
1000hrs
1443hrs
1907hrs

0600hrs
0700hrs
0900hrs
1000hrs
1025hrs
1050hrs
1331hrs
1445hrs
1545hrs
1705hrs
2130hrs

PACIFIC OCEAN

Midway Island

1. *Kaga*, *Soryu* and *Akagi* bombed.
2. *Hiryu* launches first strike.
3. *Yorktown* attacked by *Hiryu* dive-bombers.
4. *Hiryu* launches second strike.
5. *Yorktown* attacked by *Hiryu* torpedo aircraft.
6. *Hiryu* spotted by *Yorktown* aircraft.
7. TF-16 launches strike against *Hiryu*.
8. *Hiryu* bombed by *Enterprise* and *Yorktown* aircraft.
9. TF-16 recovers strike.

Japanese forces
Hiryu first strike
Hiryu second strike
Task Force 16 (Spruance)
Task Force 17 (Fletcher)
US flight paths

50 miles
50km
0
0

The ensuing attack by the remaining seven carrier bombers was one of the most accurate of the entire war and fully confirmed the elite status of the *Hiryu*'s Carrier Bomber Unit. Of the seven aircraft, three scored direct hits and two scored damaging near-misses. Of the seven that dived, going down to below 1,000ft to ensure hits, five survived to return to *Hiryu*. The first hit, scored by the first aircraft to attack, was by a high-explosive bomb near the Number 2 elevator aft of the island. It penetrated to the hangar deck and started a small fire. The second aircraft missed, but its bomb landed close enough astern to start fires on the fantail. Both of the first two aircraft were shot down by antiaircraft fire.

The second hit, scored at 1214hrs by the fifth carrier bomber to attack, was by far the most damaging. The 250kg semi-armor-piercing bomb landed just inboard of the island amidships. It exploded in the stack uptakes, creating havoc in the firerooms and slowing the ship to six knots. The sixth carrier bomber to attack circled forward of *Yorktown* and conducted a shallow glide-bomb attack. Its weapon, a 250kg semi-armor-piercing bomb, hit the Number 1 elevator and exploded deep in the hull, starting fires. The last attacker dropped its bomb from the starboard beam and scored a near miss. By any measure, three hits and two near misses by seven aircraft was an impressive achievement.

At the end of the attack, *Hiryu*'s Carrier Bomber Unit had been shattered: 13 of 18 carrier bombers had been shot down with three Zero fighters also lost. The cost to the defending CAP was a single fighter. However, at the end of the attack, *Yorktown* had come to a stop and was issuing thick, black smoke from the bomb hole amidships. Kobayashi's airmen had seemingly dealt the American carrier serious damage. At 1323hrs, Fletcher shifted his flag to the cruiser *Astoria*, and Spruance dispatched two cruisers and two destroyers from TF-16 to assist *Yorktown*.

In the immediate aftermath of the Japanese dive-bombing attack on *Yorktown*, corpsmen treat casualties in the area aft of the island. In the background is the Number 4 1.1in. gun mount. (US Naval Historical Center)

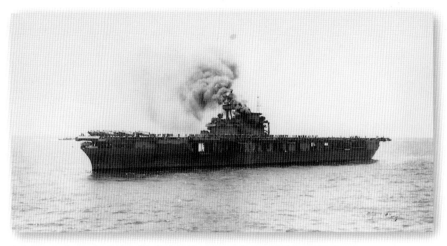

TOMONAGA ATTACKS *YORKTOWN*

Yamaguchi withheld from committing *Hiryu*'s carrier attack aircraft until the situation was clarified. He knew the only chance to get the Midway operation back on track was to sink or at least disable the three American carriers. Quick and effective action by *Hiryu* still presented a chance to save the situation. At 1245hrs, one of *Hiryu*'s returning carrier bombers radioed that the strike of *Hiryu*'s Carrier Bomber Unit had left one American carrier burning. With this knowledge, Yamaguchi knew that *Hiryu* still faced two operational American carriers. For the next strike, Yamaguchi possessed few resources. *Hiryu*'s Carrier Attack Aircraft Unit had participated in the morning strike on Midway and had fared badly. Of the 18 aircraft, only eight remained fully serviceable. Yamaguchi received a welcome boost when at 1130hrs one of *Akagi*'s carrier attack planes assigned to conduct morning search duties recovered on *Hiryu*. By 1245hrs, the strike was ready. It was a makeshift force of 16 aircraft: nine *Hiryu* carrier attack planes, one from *Akagi*, escorted by six Zero fighters, four from *Hiryu* and two from *Kaga*. The strike was led by Tomonaga, leader of both *Hiryu*'s Air Group and of the morning strike on Midway. Tomonaga's aircraft was damaged on the left wing during the morning strike. The holes were patched, but adequate time was not available to repair the leaking fuel tanks. Other pilots offered to exchange aircraft with Tomonaga, but he refused, virtually ensuring he would not be able to return to *Hiryu*. Yamaguchi ordered Tomonaga to hit one of the undamaged American carriers.

At 1315hrs, the remnants of *Hiryu*'s first strike returned. Following the recovery, Yamaguchi immediately launched Tomonaga's aircraft. At 1331hrs they departed to the east. At this point, TF-17 was just 83 miles away and TF-16 only 112 miles distant.

By the time Tomonaga's strike began its flight, *Yorktown*'s crew had put out the fires and restored the boilers to enable the carrier to steam at 25 knots. At about 1430hrs, when Tomonaga sighted a US carrier task force at some 35 miles away with one seemingly intact carrier, five cruisers, and 12 destroyers steaming at 24 knots to the east, he had no idea this was the previously damaged *Yorktown*. He immediately ordered an attack.

The Americans were already aware of Tomonaga's approach. The cruiser *Pensacola* (a reinforcement from TF-16) gained radar contact at 1427hrs on a group of unidentified aircraft 45 miles to the northwest. A few minutes later,

Yorktown gained contact at 33 miles. When the second group of Japanese raiders appeared, only six Wildcats were overhead. At 1429hrs, four of these fighters were ordered to proceed to the northwest at 10,000ft to intercept the oncoming Japanese; two minutes later the last two fighters were vectored to the northwest at 7,000ft. With all available fighters now proceeding to intercept, the fighter direction officer requested reinforcements from TF-16's 15 fighters aloft at 1430hrs. Eight more were vectored from TF-16 to reinforce *Yorktown*'s defenses.

After spotting the American carrier, Tomonaga ordered a gentle dive from altitude to gain air speed. Approaching from *Yorktown*'s port quarter, Tomonaga split his force into two groups of five; each would sweep ahead of the target and conduct an anvil attack.

Compared with the interception of *Hiryu*'s dive-bombers, the air battle against *Hiryu*'s torpedo bombers did not go as well for the Americans. Several factors conspired to allow most of the attacking force to launch their weapons at *Yorktown*. These included an inadequate number of fighters deployed at improper altitudes and a much more effective close escort by the Japanese fighters.

By 1436hrs, the fighter direction officer ordered the four fighters sent out at 10,000ft to return to *Yorktown*. They had missed *Hiryu*'s low-flying carrier attack planes in the clouds. However, the two fighters at 7,000ft were able to find the approaching Japanese and caught a section of the carrier attack planes by surprise. One carrier attack plane was destroyed before the escorting Zero fighters succeeded in flaming both Wildcats.

The pilots of VF-3, spotted on *Yorktown*'s deck, were eager to get in the air to defend their carrier. At 1440hrs they were launched in the midst of the Japanese attack but all were low on fuel and had no time to gain speed or altitude. At the same time, Tomonaga signaled his remaining nine aircraft to commence their attack. The carrier attack planes went to their attack altitude of 200ft at a speed of 200 knots.

Tomonaga's attack group races toward *Yorktown*. This view was taken from the heavy cruiser *Pensacola*. The four carrier attack aircraft can be seen just above the bursts of 5in. shells in the middle of the picture. Since only four carrier attack aircraft approached *Yorktown* from *Pensacola*'s position in the screen, the aircraft to the far left must be a fighter, either Japanese or American. (US Naval Historical Center)

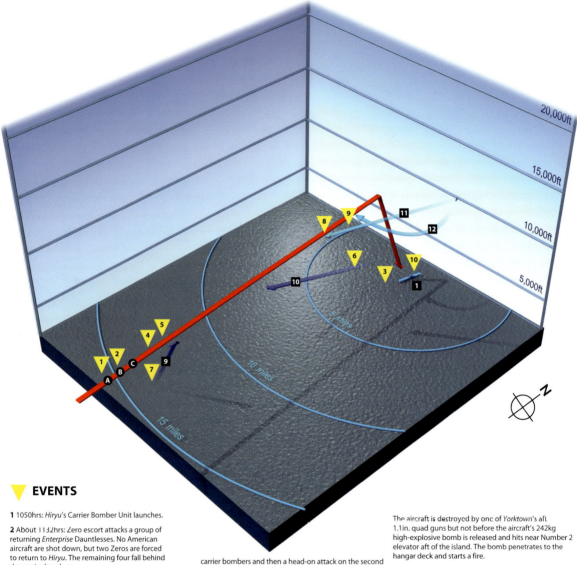

▼ EVENTS

1 1050hrs: *Hiryu*'s Carrier Bomber Unit launches.

2 About 1132hrs: Zero escort attacks a group of returning *Enterprise* Dauntlesses. No American aircraft are shot down, but two Zeros are forced to return to *Hiryu*. The remaining four fall behind the carrier bombers.

3 1150hrs: *Yorktown* launches 12 Wildcats as CAP relief.

4 1151hrs: *Hiryu* attack group detected by *Yorktown* radar bearing 255 degrees at 32 miles.

5 1155hrs: *Hiryu* attack group spots TF-17 25 miles (40km) away.

6 1156hrs: seven Wildcats (six from Fourth Division and one from Second Division) head down 255 degrees bearing to intercept Japanese.

7 1158hrs: remainder of Second Division Wildcats sent to intercept.

8 1200hrs: Kobayashi radios *Hiryu* that he is attacking.

9 1200–1209hrs: *Yorktown* CAP intercepts *Hiryu* carrier bombers. In the first part of the fight, five Wildcats conduct a slashing attack on the one group of nine

carrier bombers and then a head-on attack on the second group of nine. The Japanese formation is shattered. The Japanese fighters do not intervene until late in the engagement when the damage is already done. Three Zeros are shot down for the loss of a single Wildcat. Eight carrier bombers survive to approach *Yorktown*. One group of three heads east toward *Yorktown* and another group of five circles to the southwest to approach from out of the sun. The latter group encounters the Wildcats from VF-8 and loses one aircraft within five miles of *Yorktown*. The Wildcats from VF-6 also spot this group, but their attempted interception is unsuccessful.

10 1209hrs: *Yorktown* sights the Japanese aircraft closing from astern and from starboard quarter.

11 1210hrs: unknown Japanese pilot signals he is attacking.

12 1211hrs: first carrier bomber piloted by an unknown aviator holds its dive to well under 1,000ft to ensure a hit.

The aircraft is destroyed by one of *Yorktown*'s aft 1.1in. quad guns but not before the aircraft's 242kg high-explosive bomb is released and hits near Number 2 elevator aft of the island. The bomb penetrates to the hangar deck and starts a fire.

13 1211hrs: second carrier bomber, also piloted by an unknown aviator, is destroyed by antiaircraft fire and crashes in *Yorktown*'s wake. The detonation of the aircraft's bomb scatters fragments on *Yorktown*'s fantail and starts small fires.

14 1211hrs: third carrier bomber, piloted by Petty Officer 2nd Class Tsuchiya, misses astern and escapes.

15 About 1214hrs: fourth carrier bomber, piloted by Warrant Officer Matsumoto, misses astern and escapes.

16 1214hrs: second hit scored by 250kg semi-armor-piercing bomb just inboard of the island amidships. This aircraft was flown by Warrant Officer Nakazawa. His bomb explodes in the ship's stack uptakes, damaging uptakes for three firerooms and extinguishing fires in another three. *Yorktown*'s speed falls to six knots with thick, black smoke being issued from a hole amidships. Nakazawa survives.

THE JAPANESE RESPONSE

Dive-bombers from carrier *Hiryu* attack *Yorktown* on the afternoon of June 4.

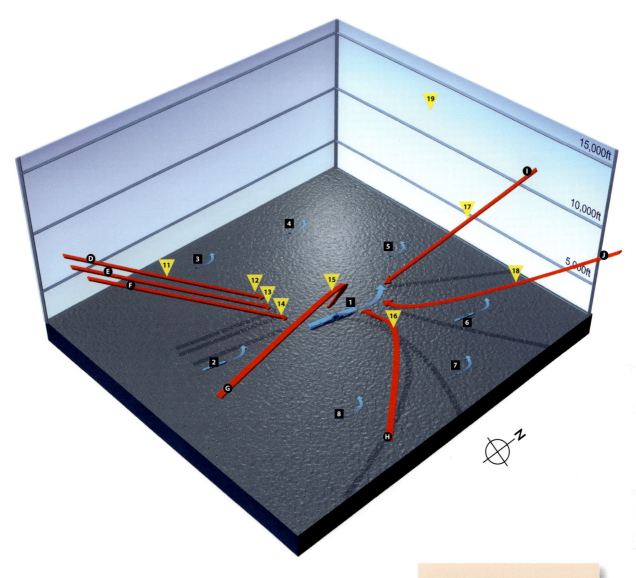

17 1215hrs: sixth carrier bomber, piloted by Warrant Officer Nakagawa, circles forward of *Yorktown* and conducts a shallow glide-bomb attack. Nakagawa scores a hit with a 250kg semi-armor-piercing bomb on the Number 1 elevator and explodes deep in the ship's hull starting fires. Nakagawa returns to *Hiryu*.

18 1215hrs: seventh carrier bomber, piloted by Petty Officer 1st Class Seo, attacks from starboard beam and scores a near miss. He also survives.

19 1239hrs: last Japanese aircraft shot down. Thirteen of 18 carrier bombers are shot down with three Zero fighters for the loss of one Wildcat.

US FORCES
1 *Yorktown*
2 *Astoria*
3 *Hammann*
4 *Hughes*
5 *Anderson*
6 *Portland*
7 *Russell*
8 *Morris*
9 VF-3 Second Division CAP (six F4Fs)
10 VF-3 Fourth Division CAP (six F4Fs)
11 VF-8 CAP augmentation (four F4Fs)
12 VF-6 CAP augmentation (four F4Fs)

JAPANESE FORCES
A *Hiryu* Carrier Bomber Unit (1st *Chutai*) (nine D3A1 dive-bombers)
B *Hiryu* Carrier Bomber Unit (2nd *Chutai*) (nine D3A1 dive-bombers)
C *Hiryu* Fighter Escort (four Zero fighters)
D D3A1 Type 99 Carrier Bombers (pilot unknown)
E D3A1 Type 99 Carrier Bombers (pilot unknown)
F D3A1 Type 99 Carrier Bombers (pilot Petty Officer 2nd Class Tsuchiya)
G D3A1 Type 99 Carrier Bombers (pilot Warrant Officer Matsumoto)
H D3A1 Type 99 Carrier Bombers (pilot Warrant Officer Nakazawa)
I D3A1 Type 99 Carrier Bombers (pilot Warrant Officer Nakagawa)
J D3A1 Type 99 Carrier Bombers (pilot Petty Officer 1st Class Seo)

The second *chutai* under Lieutenant Hashimoto making its attack on *Yorktown*. Two Type 97 carrier attack planes are visible – one above *Yorktown* and one astern. Both have already dropped their torpedoes. Of the five aircraft in Hashimoto's *chutai*, two scored hits. (US Naval Historical Center)

BOTTOM

The moment of impact of the first torpedo to hit *Yorktown*. Another torpedo would hit seconds later. It is important to note that every time a US carrier was hit by a torpedo in the carrier battles of 1942, the carrier ended up being lost. (US Naval Historical Center)

Tomonaga's section of four aircraft penetrated the screen aft of *Pensacola*. At their approach, *Yorktown* turned hard starboard away from Tomonaga's aircraft. In response, Tomonaga's aircraft split up to get in launch positions. The first fighter off *Yorktown*'s deck, flown by the redoubtable Thach, immediately spotted a Japanese aircraft after launch. Thach flamed the aircraft, but its pilot was able to hold the burning plane level and make an excellent torpedo drop. This was Tomonaga, but his skill and bravery went unrewarded when his torpedo missed. Tomonaga's wingman also missed, but survived the attack only to be shot down later by TF-16 fighters arriving from the south. The other two aircraft from Tomonaga's section attempted attacks from *Yorktown*'s port side. Both were shot down by either newly launched VF-3 fighters or by antiaircraft fire. One launched its torpedo and missed; the other jettisoned its weapon.

The sacrifice of Tomonaga and his four aircraft set up the successful attack by the second section of five carrier attack planes. These entered the formation in a gap between cruiser *Portland* and destroyer *Balch* and headed toward

Yorktown's port bow. *Yorktown* tried to turn to starboard to present its stern to the attackers, but the ship could not turn fast enough. At 150ft, the Japanese aircraft approached *Yorktown* under heavy fire and fighter attack. One of the scrambled VF-3 fighters attempted to attack the carrier attack planes, but was engaged by two Zeros. In turn, two Wildcats intervened and shot down both Japanese fighters. This prompted the section of *Kaga* Zeros to enter the fray. While the fighters were dueling, all five carrier attack planes survived several attacks by Wildcats to reach their launch positions. The section leader and three others set off their torpedoes, but the release system of the lone *Akagi* attack plane failed to operate. Of the four torpedoes, some launched only 600 yards away, two found their target. Both hit the port side with devastating effect. Three firerooms and the forward generator room were flooded and all boilers were knocked off line. *Yorktown* came to a halt and took an immediate 23-degree list.

A Japanese Type 97 carrier attack aircraft turning away from *Yorktown* after launching its torpedo. The aircraft is being viewed from one of *Yorktown*'s 20mm gun positions. A thin plume of smoke can be seen trailing from the plane's port wing root. (US Naval Historical Center)

EVENTS

1 1445hrs: *Hiryu* spotted by VS-5 aircraft.

2 1525hrs: *Enterprise* begins launch of composite strike group composed of 25 Dauntlesses from three different squadrons. One aborts after launch.

3 1645hrs: the American aircraft spot the remaining units of the 1st Kido Butai some 40 miles away. The strike leader, Lieutenant Gallaher, leads his group to the southwest to launch his attack out of the afternoon sun. Gallaher orders *Enterprise*'s dive-bombers to attack the *Hiryu* and *Yorktown*'s aircraft to attack the nearest battleship (*Haruna*).

4 1701hrs: *Chikuma* spots dive-bombers and uses her antiaircraft fire to alert the CAP. A total of 13 Zeros are aloft on CAP, including a group of seven aircraft from *Soryu* and *Kaga*, another four from *Akagi*, and two from *Kaga*. The disposition and altitude of these aircraft are unknown.

5 1705hrs: The American dive-bombers begin their dives. *Hiryu* puts up a heavy concentration of antiaircraft fire and the CAP desperately attacks the Dauntlesses. *Hiryu*'s skipper puts the ship in a sharp port turn. All of these measures combine to make *Hiryu* a tough target and the first several aircraft miss their target. Upon seeing this, Shumway orders his aircraft to join the attack on *Hiryu*. Four 1,000-pound bomb hits are gained on the forward flight deck which creates large fires and blows the forward elevator against the island. The last aircraft to dive on *Hiryu* were led by Best, hero of the morning strike on *Akagi*. All told, three Dauntlesses were lost, all to fighters.

6 1720hrs: *Hornet*'s strike of 14 Dauntlesses (two aircraft aborted en route) arrives. *Hiryu* is clearly on fire and doomed, so the dive-bombers attack cruisers *Tone* and *Chikuma* without success.

7 1745–1815hrs: two groups of B-17s attack *Hiryu* and *Chikuma*. No hits are scored, but some of the B-17s are low enough to strafe *Hiryu* with machine-gun fire, inflicting several casualties.

ATTACK ON *HIRYU*

Task Force 16 launches a joint strike against the last surviving Japanese aircraft carrier.

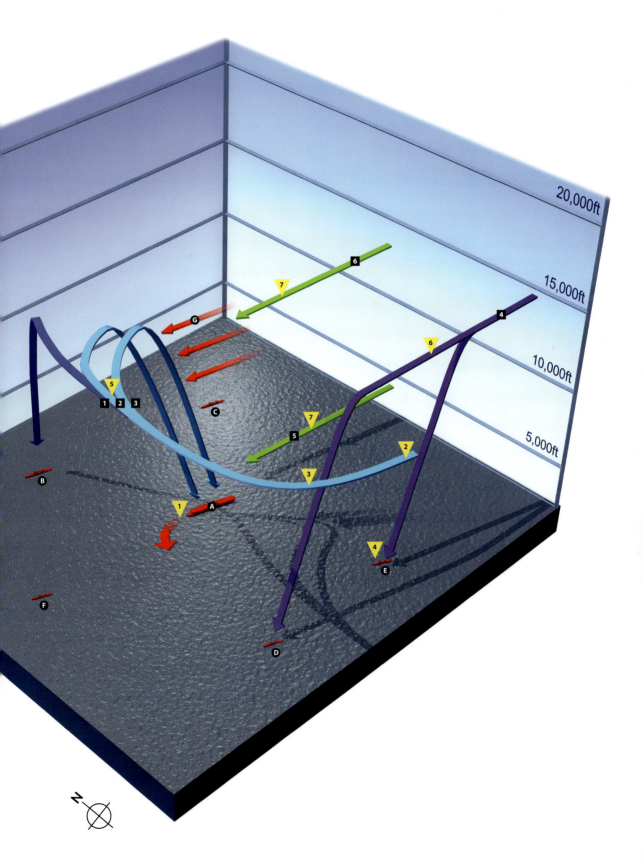

As the strike from *Enterprise* was launching, *Hiryu's* second strike against *Yorktown* returned to its ship. The remaining aircraft, five carrier attack aircraft and three fighters, landed aboard by 1540hrs. In spite of the heavy losses, the debriefing of the surviving pilots gave Yamaguchi cause for encouragement. It was assessed that three torpedo hits had been scored on a Yorktown-class carrier. With two carriers hit and damaged or sunk, this meant *Hiryu* faced only a single operative American carrier.

To hit the third and final American carrier Yamaguchi believed remained still operational, he planned a third strike at 1800hrs. The timing was key; maybe a small strike could sneak in under the cover of dusk. For this strike, *Hiryu* could muster only four carrier bombers and five carrier attack aircraft. Nine fighters were allocated as escort. To guide the attackers to their target, Yamaguchi planned to launch the D4Y1 reconnaissance plane an hour before the strike.

The encouraging situation taking shape in Yamaguchi's mind was shattered by new information received from a new wave of Japanese scout aircraft dispatched in the early afternoon. The first search aircraft did not depart until 1335hrs from *Chikuma* and two more followed from *Tone* at 1400hrs. One of these aircraft, the infamous *Tone* plane Number 4 (the originator of the frustratingly incomplete morning reports) radioed at 1550hrs that two carriers were operating in the large task force located to the northwest some 120 miles from the 1st Kido Butai.

The fact that two American carriers remained operational was soon confirmed with the arrival of a large group of American dive-bombers. *Enterprise*'s strike group, now reduced to 24 aircraft after one abort, was about to complete the immolation of the 1st Kido Butai. Upon sighting the Japanese force some 30 miles away, Lieutenant Gallaher, the strike leader, led his group to the southwest to launch his attack from out of the afternoon sun. Once again, a group of American dive-bombers arrived overhead the 1st Kido Butai and achieved complete surprise. Gallaher instructed his *Enterprise* aircraft to attack *Hiryu*; the 14 *Yorktown* dive-bombers were ordered to attack the nearest battleship.

On *Hiryu*, the deck crew was preparing to launch the pre-strike D4Y1 reconnaissance aircraft. A total of 13 Zeros were aloft on CAP, but their disposition and altitude is unknown. Once again, the Japanese were surprised by a group of American dive-bombers as it was not until 1701hrs that the Japanese spotted the Americans overhead. At 1705hrs, the American dive-bombers began their attack. Caught by surprise and with her CAP outnumbered by the attacking dive-bombers, the fate of *Hiryu* was all but sealed. The defending fighters desperately attacked the Dauntlesses as they dived, but, once in a dive, there was little chance of a successful interception. *Hiryu*'s skipper put the ship in a sharp port turn. Upon seeing the first two VS-6 aircraft miss, the skipper of VB-3 ordered his aircraft to join the attack on *Hiryu*. Four hits were gained in the area forward of the island, which created large fires and blew the forward elevator against the island. The last aircraft to dive on *Hiryu* were led by Lieutenant Best, hero of the morning strike on *Akagi*. All told, three Dauntlesses were lost, all to fighters.

Fifteen minutes later, *Hornet*'s strike arrived. *Hiryu* was clearly on fire and doomed, so the remaining 14 dive-bombers attacked her escorts. No hits were gained. One hour later, 12 B-17 bombers conducted the final attack on the 1st Kido Butai on June 4; again no hits were scored.

The four bomb hits on *Hiryu* were enough to set the ship aflame. Now *Hiryu* was to experience the death by fire that had accounted for the 1st Kido Butai's other three carriers. The bombs penetrated to the hangar deck where the small strike was being prepared for launch. The fires gained strength, and at 2123hrs, the ship went dead in the water. Both Captain Kaku and Admiral Yamaguchi decided to remain aboard. By 0430hrs on June 5, the crew was taken off. At 0510hrs, a Japanese destroyer attempted to scuttle the ship, hitting her with a single torpedo and departing the scene. This was insufficient to sink the carrier because at 0630hrs an aircraft from *Hosho* found and photographed the still-burning carrier which was observed to still have survivors onboard. Another destroyer was sent to rescue these men, but at 0912hrs *Hiryu* sank by the bow. Of the last 70 men aboard, 35 were eventually rescued by the Americans. Of *Hiryu*'s crew, 383 men were lost, not counting the prisoners of war.

THE US CARRIER AIR ATTACK OF JUNE 6 AGAINST JAPANESE HEAVY CRUISER *MIKUMA* (pp. 82–83)

Following her collision with sister ship *Mogami* early on the morning of June 5, damage to heavy cruiser *Mikuma* **(1)** was fairly light. With the more heavily damaged *Mogami* able to make only 12 knots, the two cruisers, escorted by two destroyers, headed west to depart the battle area. This scene shows the first of the American air attacks on the cruisers. At 0630hrs, a PBY from Midway spotted the small Japanese force. The two cruisers were reported as "battleships" and in response what was left of Marine squadron VMSB-241 was dispatched from Midway to attack this lucrative target. Included in the attack were 12 dive-bombers – six Dauntlesses and six of the older SB2U Vindicators. The six Dauntlesses attacked *Mogami*, but against heavy antiaircraft fire, no hits were scored. The six Vindicators, under Captain Richard Fleming, went after *Mikuma*. Fleming decided to execute a glide-bombing attack from 4,000ft. Again, the antiaircraft fire was heavy and Fleming's aircraft was hit. As shown in the scene, it crashed into the sea with no survivors **(2)**. Despite persistent myth, Fleming's aircraft did not crash on *Mikuma*'s No. 4 turret. None of the Vindicators scored a hit, and a B-17 attack later in the day was also without success. However, the luck of the two cruisers ran out the next day when Navy Dauntlesses attacked them.

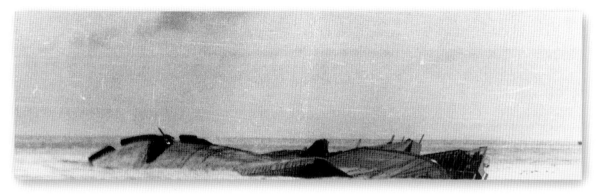

YORKTOWN'S ORDEAL

Compared with the desperate but ineffective attempts to save the Japanese carriers struck on June 4, superior damage-control practices and efforts almost succeeded in saving *Yorktown*. At 1455hrs on June 4, Captain Buckmaster ordered the ship to be abandoned. The ship still had a severe list as a result of the two torpedo hits and Buckmaster feared the entire crew could be lost if the ship capsized. By 1639hrs, escorts picked up all crew members in the water, aided by calm conditions. After transferring to cruiser *Astoria*, Fletcher ordered TF-17 at 1712hrs to the southeast to join Spruance, leaving *Yorktown* unattended. Later, he changed his mind and assigned a single destroyer to guard the listing carrier. Fletcher planned to return the next morning to evaluate the prospects of salvaging the ship. The drifting *Yorktown* was spotted by two different Japanese search planes during the afternoon.

On June 5, Buckmaster collected a salvage party of 170 men and placed them aboard three destroyers sent to rejoin the carrier, arriving at 1800hrs. Salvage efforts began to gain steam on June 6 with Buckmaster's salvage party conducting counterflooding and jettisoning anything loose topside. It appeared these efforts were going to pay off when the fleet tug *Vireo* showed up in the early afternoon and began a slow tow of the carrier to Pearl Harbor. However, Yamamoto had already ordered submarine *I-168* to the scene to ensure the carrier did not escape. In a well-executed attack at 1336hrs, *I-168* fired a full salvo at *Yorktown* from only 1,300 yards. Two torpedoes hit the carrier and a third hit the destroyer *Hammann* laying alongside and broke it in half. After this attack, *Yorktown* was again abandoned at 1555hrs, this time for good. At 0501hrs the next morning she sank.

SPRUANCE'S BATTLE

Even after his transfer to the cruiser *Astoria*, Fletcher remained in overall command of the two American task forces. At 1811hrs on June 4, Spruance asked his superior, "Have you any instructions for further operations?" When Fletcher replied "Negative. Will conform to your movements," tactical command was assumed by Spruance and he conducted the rest of battle without reference to Fletcher. This was a selfless act by Fletcher which guaranteed continuity of command for TF-16, but also has served to minimize the role Fletcher played in achieving victory. From this point, Spruance's primary concern was not to be lured into a surface engagement with superior Japanese forces while using his remaining air power to strike

Yorktown sinking on the morning of June 7, as seen from one of her escorting destroyers. Note the large torpedo hole in the hull. In 1998, the ship was discovered by explorer Robert Ballard in an almost upright position some 17,000ft below. (US Naval Historical Center)

targets of opportunity while still covering Midway from possible invasion. At 1915hrs, Spruance ordered TF-16 to steam to the east to avoid any Japanese force possibly advancing to the east. At midnight, Spruance took TF-16 to the north but was forced to continue east until 0200hrs on June 5 after a false radar contact on a surface target. By 0420hrs on June 5, TF-16 was heading to the southwest to be within range of Midway in the morning.

The morning of June 5 found TF-16 in a band of bad weather. Just as Fletcher had done the day before, Spruance decided to wait for the results of Midway's morning scouting missions before deciding what to do. However, a series of PBY reports throughout the day served only to confuse the issue and even suggested the possibility of a fifth Japanese carrier. By 1100hrs, Spruance was confident that no immediate threat existed against Midway so he took TF-16 to the northwest at 25 knots to investigate the carrier reports received that morning. He planned a long-range strike with his remaining dive-bombers that afternoon.

Hornet launched a strike of 12 dive-bombers at 1512hrs led by Ring against a target 240 miles away. A second deckload of 14 dive-bombers from VS-8 was launched 30 minutes later. Ring's luck was no better on June 5 than the day before. He led his strike out to 315 miles and found nothing. On the way back, he came across a Japanese "light cruiser" which he attacked without success. The target was actually the destroyer *Tanikaze* which Nagumo had dispatched to make sure *Hiryu* had sunk. *Hornet*'s second wave made no contact.

Enterprise's contribution to the futile American efforts of June 5 was a composite strike of 32 Dauntlesses from the four different dive-bomber squadrons now aboard *Enterprise*. This strike departed around 1530hrs and flew some 265 miles out to the northwest with no contact. When the strike leader heard Ring's report of a light cruiser, he took his 32 aircraft to hit the same target. However, *Enterprise*'s dive-bombers were no more successful at hitting the adroitly maneuvering destroyer. *Tanikaze* even succeeded in shooting down a VS-5 Dauntless. In addition to the efforts of the Dauntlesses

After TF-16's attacks on June 6, two reconnaissance Dauntlesses were launched from *Enterprise* to record the condition of *Mikuma*. The result was some of the most enduring pictures of the Pacific War. In this view, *Mikuma* is shown in her death throes. The ship is on fire and the devastation from behind the stack to her rear 8in. turrets is total. The guns of her Number 3 8in. gun turret are askew, the result of the first bomb to hit the ship. (US Naval Historical Center)

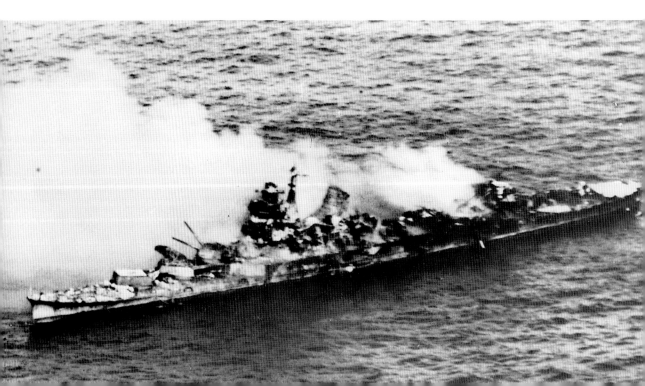

The pursuit phase: June 5–6

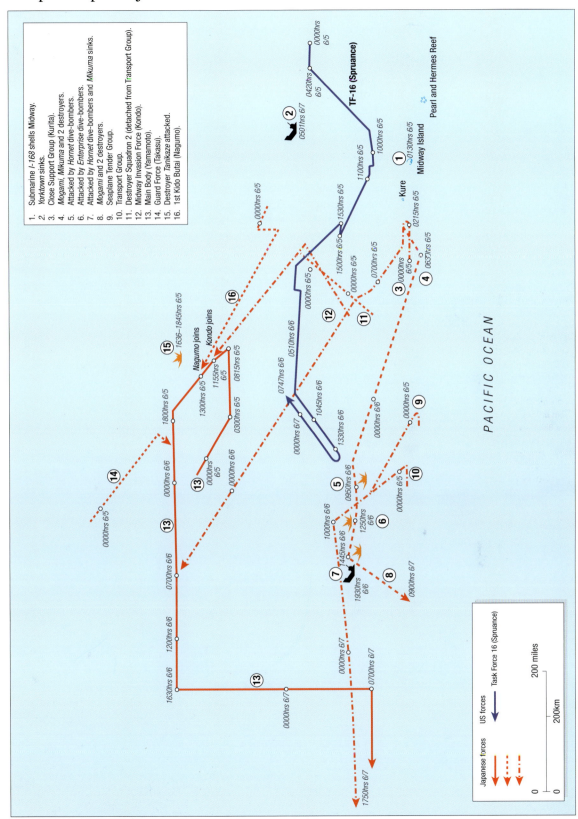

1. Submarine *I-168* shells Midway.
2. *Yorktown* sinks.
3. Close Support Group (Kurita).
4. *Mogami*, *Mikuma* and 2 destroyers.
5. Attacked by *Hornet* dive-bombers.
6. Attacked by *Enterprise* dive-bombers.
7. Attacked by *Hornet* dive-bombers and *Mikuma* sinks.
8. *Mogami* and 2 destroyers.
9. Seaplane Tender Group.
10. Transport Group.
11. Destroyer Squadron 2 (detached from Transport Group).
12. Midway Invasion Force (Kondo).
13. Main Body (Yamamoto).
14. Guard Force (Takasu).
15. Destroyer *Tanikaze* attacked.
16. 1st Kido Butai (Nagumo).

TF-16 (Spruance)

Pearl and Hermes Reef

Midway Island

Kure

PACIFIC OCEAN

Nagumo joins

Kondo joins

Japanese forces

US forces

Task Force 16 (Spruance)

200 miles

200km

87

to hit the destroyer, 18 B-17s attacked the Japanese ship in two different groups during the afternoon. *Tanikaze* suffered no direct hits, but six crewmen were killed in the attacks. In return, aside from the Dauntless shot down, another was lost operationally and two B-17s failed to return.

THE PURSUIT PHASE

When the Midway operation was cancelled, the most exposed Japanese forces were the four heavy cruisers of Kurita's Close Support Group. Unfortunately for Kurita, the orders canceling his bombardment of Midway were misrouted and he did not receive them until approximately 0230hrs on the morning of June 5. By this time, Midway was only some 50 miles away. The Japanese cruisers turned away, but during the course change an American submarine was spotted. Executing emergency evasion, heavy cruiser *Mogami* smashed into her sister ship *Mikuma*. *Mikuma* was only lightly damaged but *Mogami*'s bow was smashed and she could proceed only at 12 knots. Being so close to the airbase at Midway, her survival seemed doubtful. Kurita ordered his other two cruisers to maintain their high speed transit to the west, leaving *Mikuma* to escort the crippled *Mogami*.

As Spruance's carriers chased reports of phantom carriers on June 5, Midway's aircraft were ordered to deal with the two "battleships" reported close to the island. These were actually Kurita's two heavy cruisers steaming slowly to the west. On June 5, 12 Midway dive-bombers and eight B-17s were sent against the cruisers, but no hits were scored.

Taken from the cruiser's port quarter, this shot of *Mikuma* shows the extensive damage amidships. The mainmast is completely missing and half of the stack is gone. After the battle, a myth took hold that a Vindicator dive-bomber, flown by Captain Richard Fleming, United States Marine Corps, crashed onto *Mikuma*, with the wreckage seen on top of No. 4 turret used as evidence. In fact, Fleming crashed into the sea. (US Naval Historical Center)

The morning of June 6 found TF-16 heading west. At 0500hrs, Spruance's carriers were 350 miles northwest of Midway. *Enterprise* launched 18 Dauntlesses to conduct a 180-degree morning search to the west out to 200 miles. At 0645hrs, one of the scout aircraft reported a force of one battleship, one cruiser, and three destroyers only some 130 miles to the southwest of TF-16. The report was garbled and it was received by Spruance as one carrier and five destroyers. At 0730hrs, the same aircraft dropped a message on *Enterprise*'s deck with a report of two cruisers and two destroyers, but located to the southeast of the previous report. Spruance took this to be two different groups and decided it was worth a full strike. What his pilots had actually spotted were *Mikuma* and *Mogami*, escorted by two destroyers, limping to the west.

Hornet mounted a strike of 26 dive-bombers, escorted by eight fighters, and launched at 0800hrs. The urgency was much reduced when *Enterprise* recovered the morning scout aircraft including the pilot who made the morning reports. He confirmed that no carrier was present.

Leading *Hornet*'s strike, Ring finally got his chance to inflict damage on the Japanese. Just before the 1000hrs, his aircraft placed two bomb hits on *Mogami*. In exchange, two Dauntlesses were shot down. The ordeal of the two Japanese cruisers was far from over. *Enterprise* launched a strike of 31 dive-bombers and three torpedo planes escorted by 12 Wildcats at 1045hrs. The Dauntlesses concentrated on *Mikuma* which they had identified as a battleship. The undamaged cruiser took five direct hits and two near misses, engulfing the ship in fire and smoke and forcing it to go dead in the water. At 1358hrs, the fires spread to the torpedo room aft, and several of

Some of the engineering personnel from *Hiryu* were left behind after the crew abandoned ship early on June 5. They were later able to find an exit from the engineering spaces and launched one of *Hiryu*'s boats. The ship's engineer and 38 others drifted for 14 days before being rescued by seaplane tender *Ballard* on 19 June. Of the 39, 34 survived to be taken prisoner. (US Naval Historical Center)

The stern of destroyer *Hammann* going down, as viewed from *Yorktown*. After being struck by one of *I-168*'s torpedoes, the destroyer sank within four minutes with heavy loss of life. (US Naval Historical Center)

the huge weapons exploded, wrecking the aft section of the ship. As the remaining crew was abandoning ship, a third wave of American dive-bombers appeared. This was the second strike of the day from *Hornet*, this one with 24 dive-bombers. By this point, TF-16 was only 90 miles from its target. Destroyer *Arashio* was hit by a bomb aft, killing 37 men including many *Mikuma* survivors. Destroyer *Asashio* lost 22 men to strafing. Another hit was scored on *Mogami*, but she maintained power and escaped to rendezvous with Kondo the next day. Her losses included 90 dead and 101 wounded. There was no saving *Mikuma*; she sank at approximately 1930hrs with 700 of her crew unaccounted for.

By the evening of June 6, TF-16 was within 700 miles of Wake Island. Just after 1900hrs, Spruance took TF-16 to the northeast to refuel. The battle was over.

THE ACCOUNTING

Despite the attempts by the IJN to hide the extent of the disaster from its own population and the IJA, there was no disguising the fact that the Japanese had been dealt a major defeat. The 1st Kido Butai had fought unsupported and took the brunt of Japanese losses. All four of its carriers had been sunk and all aircraft on those ships (248 in total) had been lost. As bad as the losses in aircraft were, losses in aircrew were heavy, but not as catastrophic as is commonly believed. A total of 110 aircrew were killed, with the heaviest losses from *Hiryu*'s Air Group, the result of its three strikes on June 4. By comparison, aircrew losses at the inconclusive carrier battle at Eastern Solomons fought in August 1942 also totaled 110 aircrew. Losses at the carrier battle of Santa Cruz in October 1942 accounted for 145 Japanese aircrew, including a high proportion of experienced senior leaders. Total Japanese dead were 3,057 personnel, most from the crews of the four carriers. Most significant among the carrier crew casualties was the loss of 721 aircraft technicians aboard the four carriers. In addition to the losses to the IJN's carrier force, heavy cruiser *Mikuma* was sunk and heavy cruiser *Mogami* so badly damaged that she would not be operational again until 1943. Several other smaller ships were damaged, none severely. The landing on Midway was never attempted. The only undisputed success of the whole undertaking was the capture of Attu and Kiska islands in the Aleutians on June 7.

For the Americans, the cost of inflicting a strategic defeat on the Japanese was relatively small. The most important loss to the Pacific Fleet was carrier *Yorktown*. The only other ship lost was destroyer *Hammann*. A total of 144 aircraft were lost and 362 sailors, Marines, and airmen were killed.

THE AFTERMATH

By the time TF-16 returned to Pearl Harbor on June 13, it was obvious that Nimitz's gamble had delivered one of the most important victories in American naval history. In one encounter, the Pacific Fleet had blunted the offensive strength of the Imperial Japanese Navy. The loss of Nagumo's four carriers altered the balance of power in the Pacific. Only two Japanese fleet carriers remained to act as the centerpiece of a rebuilt carrier force. The Pacific Fleet possessed three fleet carriers, soon to be joined by a fourth, *Wasp*, from the Atlantic Fleet. Before Midway, the Japanese had the advantage of a numerically superior carrier force. After Midway, this advantage had been squandered.

Without doubt, Midway was one of the most important battles in naval history. It clearly defined the course of the next stage of the Pacific War. It marked the end of the Japanese expansion phase in the Pacific War, as the events of June 4 ruined the IJN as a force capable of strategic offensive operations. The effects of the battle did not mean the end of the IJN as a fighting force, but it did wrest the initiative away from the Japanese. The Americans were quicker to respond to the changed circumstances than the Japanese by launching their first strategic offensive of the war – an attack against the Japanese-held islands of Tulagi and Guadalcanal in August. Though not a single dramatic battle like Midway, the ensuing campaign for Guadalcanal was strategically more devastating for the Japanese. The campaign would cost them only a single light carrier, among other ships, but losses to both carrier-based and land-based naval aviation units were crippling and accounted for the majority of Japan's remaining elite pre-war trained naval aircrew. While Midway ensured the Japanese could no longer go on the strategic offensive, Guadalcanal demonstrated that the remaining strength of the IJN was inadequate to prevent an American advance. The attrition at Guadalcanal through 1942 and in the remainder of the Solomons into 1943, combined with the tremendous wartime growth of the US Navy, meant that the IJN was powerless to stop the gradual American advance to the home islands.

However, by August 1942 in the immediate aftermath of Midway when the battle for Guadalcanal began, the IJN was far from a beaten force. In fact, it still outnumbered the Pacific Fleet in all categories of combatants. Six Japanese carriers would fight in the Guadalcanal campaign (two fleet carriers, two converted carriers of the Junyo class, and two light carriers) against four American carriers. Of the two carrier battles during the campaign, one (Eastern Solomons) was an inconclusive draw, and the other, Santa Cruz, was a Japanese tactical victory. However, with the loss of the four fleet carriers at

One of the iconic images of the battle and the entire Pacific War features SBD Dauntless dive-bombers over a burning ship. The ship is the heavy cruiser *Mikuma* and the date is June 6. (US Naval Historical Center)

Midway, the Japanese lacked the capabilities to follow up on any tactical advantage gained. In addition to the ability of the IJN's rebuilt carrier force to more than hold its own, Japanese surface forces were able to deal some stunning blows to the Americans at Guadalcanal.

So was Midway a decisive battle? If decisive carries the implication of changing the course of the war or in some way determining its outcome, then it is hard to declare Midway as a decisive battle. The Japanese did recover from Midway, and through 1942 retained at least parity with the Pacific Fleet and dealt the Americans several sharp reverses. Midway was the high water mark for the Japanese, but it was not the decisive factor in shaping the outcome of the war.

Nor was Midway even the largest carrier battle in the war. In June 1944, the Japanese had assembled a force of nine carriers to challenge the growing power of the Pacific Fleet. The final clash of carriers came during the American invasion of the Marianas Islands. By this time, the American Fast Carrier Force had grown to 15 carriers – eight fleet (including the veteran *Enterprise*) and seven light carriers. The numerical growth of the American carrier force had been matched with a concurrent increase in the numbers and quality of aircraft and aircrew and a new doctrine to employ them to full advantage. The transformational qualities of this combination was displayed to full effect at the battle of the Philippine Sea during which three Japanese carriers were sunk and the entire Japanese naval aviation strength virtually destroyed for relatively minor American losses. This also serves to underscore the real impact of Midway. Beginning in 1943, 14 Essex-class carriers saw combat service before the end of the war, reinforced by nine very useful Independence-class light carriers converted from light cruisers. Even had the Japanese carrier force gained victory at Midway, it would have been destroyed by the future American carrier force created by the tide of American industrial production combined with American technical and doctrinal advancements.

FURTHER READING

Many books have been published on Midway. Few are not laden with persistent myths and even fewer make use of reliable Japanese sources. The titles below are recommended for additional research into the battle.

Bicheno, Hugh, *Midway* Cassell and Company: London, 2001

Cressman, Robert J. et al., *A Glorious Page in Our History* Pictorial Histories Publishing Company: Missoula, MT, 1990

Dull, Paul S., *A Battle History of the Imperial Japanese Navy 1941–45* Naval Institute Press: Annapolis, MD, 1978

Fuchida, Mitsuo, and Okumiya, Masatake, *Midway* Naval Institute Press: Annapolis, MD, 1955

Isom, Dallas Woodbury, *Midway Inquest* Indiana University Press: Bloomington, IN, 2007

Lundstrom, John B., *The First Team* Naval Institute Press: Annapolis, MD, 1984

_____, *Black Shoe Carrier Admiral* Naval Institute Press: Annapolis, MD, 2006

Morison, Samuel Eliot, *Coral Sea, Midway and Submarine Actions May 1942– August 1942* (Volume IV of *The History of United States Naval Operations in World War II*) Little, Brown and Company: Boston, 1975

Parshall, Jonathan and Tully, Anthony, *Shattered Sword* Potomac Books, Washington, DC, 2005

Prange, Gordon W., *Miracle at Midway* McGraw-Hill Book Company: New York, 1982

Smith, Peter C., *Midway: Dauntless Victory* Pen and Sword: Barnsley, 2007

Willmott, H. P., *The Barrier and the Javelin* Naval Institute Press: Annapolis, MD, 1983

Additionally, the following Osprey titles are useful for additional background:

Duel 6: *USN Carriers vs IJN Carriers* (2007)

New Vanguard 114: *US Navy Aircraft Carriers 1922–45 (Prewar classes)* (2005)

New Vanguard 109: *Imperial Japanese Navy Aircraft Carriers 1921–45* (2005)

Campaign 214: *Coral Sea 1942* (2009)

INDEX

Numbers in **bold** refer to plates, photographs and diagrams

Abe Hiroaki, Rear Adm. 59
Adak Island 37
aftermath of Midway campaign 92–93
aircraft (carrier): IJN 19, 21–22; USN 24, 25, 26, 28
see also individual types
Akagi, IJN carrier 13, 16, **16**, 17, 18, 20, **20**, 21, 43, 47, 48, 52, 77
    attack planes recovered on Hiryu 64
    scuttled 59
    strike by *Enterprise* Air Group 53–56, **54–55**, 57
    strike on *Yorktown* 69
    under attack from B-17s **49**
Akebono Maru, IJN tanker 43
Akitsushima, IJN seaplane tender **36**
Aleutians (*AL*) operation, IJN 37, 37–38, 39, 81, 91
antiaircraft/air defense, USN carrier 26–28;
    .50-cal. machine guns 27
    1.1in. machine cannon 27, **27**
    20mm Oerlikon 27–28
    5in. dual-purpose guns 27, **27**
    escort ring protection 27
    IJN carrier 20–21
Aoki Taijiro, Cpt. 13, 59
Arashi, IJN destroyer 53
Arashio, IJN destroyer 90
Astoria, USN heavy cruiser **39**, 57, 85
Attu island 91
Australia, communications with US 5, 8
Avenger torpedo-bomber, USN 28, 47, **47**

B-17s Flying Fortress bomber, USAAF 45, **39**, 48, 49, 50
    strike on *Hiryu* **74–75**
    strike on IJN Transports 43
    strike on *Mogami* and *Mikuma* 84, 88
    strike on *Tanikaze* 88;
B-26 Marauder bomber, USAAF 47
Balch, USN destroyer 68
Ballard, USN seaplane tender 89
Best, Lt. Richard 74, 77
Blenheim, RAF bomber 20
Buckmaster, Cpt. Elliott 15, 85
Buffalo F-2A fighters, USAAF 43–44

California, USN battleship **23**
captured US pilots 60
carrier battle, June 4 44–47
    decisive phase 47–58, **54–55**, **62**
    flight tracks **51**
Chikuma, IJN heavy cruiser 45, 52, 56, 77
    search plane Number 1 48
    search plane Number 5 60
chronology, Midway campaign 9–11
Close Support Group, IJN *MI* operation 13, 30, 35, 81
Coral Sea, battle of (1942) 5, 6–7, 12, 13, 14, 17, 18, 21, 22, 23, 24, 26, 27, 29, 38
    combat air patrols (CAP) 25
    lessons learned 25
    Wildcat combat experience 28
CXAM-1 radar, US 24
D4Y1 Type 2 carrier bombers, IJN 19
    reconnaissance missions 60, 76, 77
Dauntless dive-bombers, USN 21, **25**, 26, 28, **28**, 43, 47

ditching 57
    self-sealing fuel tanks 28
    strike on *Mikuma* 82–84, **93**
Devastator torpedo-bomber, USN 26, 28, **28**, 52
Doolittle Raid 7
Dutch Harbor, IJN planned strike 37, 81

Eastern Solomons, battle of (1942) 90
Enterprise, USN carrier 7, 15, 23, **28**, 40, 43, **46**, 53
    Air Group 25–26
    antiaircraft guns **27**
    assessment of strikes on *Kaga* and *Akagi* 58
    coordinating strikes 24
    Dauntless search June 6 89
    dive-bomber (VS-6/VB-6) hits on *Kaga* and *Akagi* 53–56, **54–55**, 57, 58
    dive-bomber strike on *Tanikaze* 86
    fighter controller role 27
    at Pearl Harbor **23**
    strike on *Hiryu* 73–80, **74–75**, **76**, **78–80**
    strikes on *Mogami* and *Mikuma* 89–90, **92**
    torpedo-bomber (VT-6) strike on *Kaga* **28**, 52, **54–55**, 56
    Torpedo Squadron 6 **46**
Essex-class carriers, USN 93

Fleming, Cpt. Richard 82–84, 88
Fletcher, Rear Adm. Frank Jack **5**, 14, 24–25, 27, 43, 46, 73, 86
    gives tactical command to Spruance 85
    initial reconnaissance 44–45
    launches *Yorktown* strike 50
    transfers his flag to *USS Astoria* 39, 63
Flying Boat, IJN Type 97 **36**
    PBY, USN 43, 86
    PBY reconnaissance from Midway 45
    PBY role in campaign 40
French Frigate Shoals 37, 41

Gallaher, Lt. Wilmer 74, 77
Genda Minoru, Cdr. 12–13
    planning for *MI* operation 45
Gray, Lt. James 53
Guard Force, IJN *MI* operation 30, 36, 37

Halsey, Vice Adm. William 14
Hammann, USN destroyer 85, **90**, 91
Haruna, IJN battleship 48, 73
Hashimoto, Lt. 68
Hawaii 5, 8
Henderson, Maj. Lofton 47
Hiryu, IJN carrier 13, 17, 18, **41**, 43, 44, 47, 48
    Air Group losses 90
    attacked 73–80, **74–75**, **76**, **78–80**
    Carrier Bomber Unit 60
    combat air patrols (CAP) during strikes 52, 57, 77, 80
    crew abandons ship 77
    dive-bomber strike on *Yorktown* 59, 60, 61–63, **61**, **64**, **66–67**, 72
    engineering crew POWs 89
    launching Type 99 carrier bombers **59**
    strike by B-17s 50
    torpedo-bomber strike on *Yorktown* 64–73, **65**, 68, 69, **70–72**, 76
    Type 94 fire-control systems 21
Hornet, USN carrier 7, 15, 23, 40, 43
    Air Group 25
    Air Group ordered to fly 265-degree course 46, 53

coordinating strikes 24
    dive-bomber strike on *Tanikaze* 86
    launches first strikes 46–47
    at Pearl Harbor **7**
    strike against *Hiryu* 73
    strikes on escorts 77
    strikes on *Mogami* and *Mikuma* 89, 90
    torpedo bomber strike on Soryu 52, **54–55**
    VB-8 returns to Midway 58
Hosogaya Moshiro, Vice Adm 37, 38

I-68 (later *I-168*), IJN submarine **36**, 41, 81, 85, 90
I-121, IJN submarine 41
Imperial Japanese Army (IJA) 33
Ichiki Detachment 35
Imperial Japanese Navy (IJN)
    1st Air Fleet 12, 13, 16
    6th Air Group 19
    6th Fleet 41
    air groups 17–18, 18–19
    air groups reduced launch times 18
    aircraft radios 20
    Aleutians (*AL*) operation, IJN 37, 37–38, 39, 81, 91
    antiaircraft defense 21
    approach to contact with US fleet at Midway **42**
    carrier air defense 20–21
    carrier aircraft 1–2
    carrier forces 16–18
    carrier forces after Midway campaign 92–93
    combat air patrols (CAP) 20–21
    Combined Fleet planning and overconfidence 38–39
    differing strategic aims 33–34
    fighter direction 20
    First/Second Operational Stages (*MI* planning) 33
    first strike on Midway 43–44
    lack of early warning 20
    lack of radar 20
    losses at Midway 90–91
    Midway, *MI* Operational planning 8, 33–39
    Navy code (JN-25B) 29
    objectives in Australia 33
    order of battle at Midway 29–31
    self-sealing fuel tanks 21
    superiority of fighters and torpedo bombers 21–22
Independence-class light carriers, USN 93
Invasion Force, IJN *MI* operation 13, 30, 43, 60

Junyo, IJN carrier 37
Junyo class carriers, IJN 92

K Operation, IJN 37
    abandoned 41
Kaga, IJN carrier 13, 17, **17**, 19, 28, 43, 48, 52, 69
    fire-control 21
    scuttled 59
    strike by *Enterprise* Air Group 53–56, **54–55**, 57
Kaku Tomeo, Cpt. 13, 77, 80, 81
Kido Butai (striking force), 1st 7, 13, 29, 34–35, 36, 38, 41, 43, 49, 50
    approach to contact with US fleet at Midway **42**
    combat air patrols (CAP) 47, 50, 52
    damage-control measures after USN strikes 58
    losses at Midway 90–91
    USAAF strikes from Midway 47–48
Kido Butai, 2nd 31, 36, 37

ordered south to support 1st Kido Butai 60
King, Adm. Ernest 39
Kirishima, IJN battleship **6**, 49
Kiska island 37, 91
Kobayashi Michio, Lt 59, 60, **60**, 61, 62, 64, **66–67**, 72
Kondo Nobutake, Vice Adm, 13, 81
Kure island 35
Kurita Takeo, Vice Adm, 13, 81
Kusaka Ryunosuke, Rear Adm, 12

Lexington, USN carrier 7, 22
Leyte Gulf, battle of (1944) 13
Lindsey, Lt. Cdr. Eugene 52

Main Body, IJN *MI* operation 30, 35, 36, 60, 81
Mariana Islands, US invasion of 93
Mason, Cpt. Charles P. 15
McClusky, Lt. Cdr. Clarence 46, 53–56, 57
MI (Midway) operation planning 8, 34–39
    First/Second Operational Stages 33
    submarine scouting cordon 41
Midway island 32, **34**, 81
    combat air patrols (CAP) 43
    damaged aircraft hangar **44**
    role in campaign 40
    strike against 1st Kido Butai 47–48
    strike aircraft 43–44

Mikuma, IJN heavy cruiser **82–84**, **86**, 88–90, **88**, **93**
    collision with *Mogami* 84, 88
Minesweeper Group, IJN *MI* operation 43
Mitscher, Cpt. Marc A. "Pete" 15, 25, 46, 73
Mogami, IJN heavy cruiser 88–90;
collision with *Mikuma* 84, 88
Murray, Cpt. George 15

Nagano Osami, Adm. 33, **33**
Nagara, IJN light cruiser 59, 60
Nagumo Chuichi, Vice Adm. 12, **13**, 13, 16, 29, 36, 43, 46, 73, 86, 92
    advised second Midway strike required 48
    dilemma 48–50
    efforts at forcing surface engagement 81
    hands temporary control to Abe Hiroaki 59
    inadequate search plan 49
    orders to retain air reserve 49
    reconnaissance 45, 48, 49
    transfers his flag to *Nagara* 59, 60
Nautilus, US submarine 53
    attack on *Kaga* 59
Nimitz, Adm. Chester 5, 7, **13**, **14**, 22, 24, 26, 37, 38, 92
    intelligence before Midway 8, 28–29, 45
    planning for Midway 39–40
Nowaki, IJN destroyer 49

Okada Jisaku, Cpt. 13, 59

PBY, USN flying boats *see* Flying Boats
Pearl Harbor 8, 34, 41, 43, 85, 92
    attack 12, 18, 19, 22, 35
    IJN flying boat surveillance 37
Pensacola, USN cruiser 64, 65, 68
Philippine Sea, battle of (1944) 93
"Point Luck" 40, 43
Port Moresby, New Guinea 5, 6, 7, 34
Portland, USN cruiser 68
pursuit phase (June 5–6), Midway **87**

radar 24
    and combat air patrol (CAP) allocation process 27

CXAM-1 24
Ranger, USN carrier 22
Ring, Cdr. Stanhope 46, 52, 53, 58, 86, 89
Roosevelt, President 13
Ryujo, IJN carrier 37

Sand Island, Midway 35
Santa Cruz, battle of (1942) 92
    Losses 90–1
Saratoga, USN carrier 7, 22
    Air Group 26
SB2U-3 dive-bombers, US 48
Seaplane Tender Group, IJN *MI* operation 35
Second Combined Special Naval Landing Force, IJN *MI* operation 35
Shoho, IJN light carrier 7
Shokaku, IJN carrier **22**
    Coral Sea 7, 17, 18
Soryu, IJN carrier 13, 17, **17**, 19, 25, 41, 43, 48, 52, 56
    combat air patrols (CAP) during *Yorktown's* strike 57, 58
    fire-control systems type 94 21
    sinking 58
    strike by B-17s 50
    strike by *Yorktown's* Air Group 54–55, 57, 58
Spruance, Rear Adm. Raymond 14, **14**, 24, 40, 46, 90
    changes course to avoid surface action 60
    dispatches cruisers to assist *Yorktown* 63
    given tactical command 85
    launches strike against *Hiryu* 73
    staff failures 58, 73
    strategic situation, June 1942 **4**;
submarines, role in Midway campaign 36–37

Tanaka Razio, Rear Adm. 13
Tanikaze, Japanese destroyer 86–88
Task Force 16 (TF-16), USN 24, 25, 31–32, 40, 43, 46, 53, 58, 60, 85, 89, 90, 92
Task Force 17 (TF-17), USN 24, 25, 31, 46, 50
Thatch, Cdr. John 56, 68, 72
"Tokyo Express", Guadalcanal 13
Tomonaga Joichi, Lt. 44, 48, **64**
    strike on *Yorktown* 64–68, **65**, **70–72**
Tone, IJN heavy cruiser 35, 45, **46**, 52
    search plane Number 4 48, 49, 50, 60, 77
torpedoes
    Mark XIII aerial USN 28
    Type 91 Mod 3 Air, IJN 22
Transport Group, IJN *MI* operation 13, 30 35, 43
Tsuchiya, Petty Officer **61**
Tulagi, Solomon Islands 6, 7
Type 0 float reconnaissance plane, IJN **46**
Type 2 carrier bomber, IJN 19, 60
Type 95 float reconnaissance plane, IJN **46**
Type 96 carrier aircraft, IJN 76
Type 97 ("Kate") carrier attack aircraft, IJN 22, **22**, **69**
Type 99 ("Val") carrier bomber, IJN 21

United States Navy (USN)
    air defense 26–28
    Air Groups 24–26
    aircraft 28
    approach to contact with IJN 1st Kido Butai at Midway **42**
    battleship employment 39
    carrier forces 22–24
    codebreakers knowledge of *MI* Operation 39
    communications with Australia 5, 8
    coordinating air operations 24

damage-control practices 85
    intelligence 28–29
    launch periods 24
    losses at Midway 90–91
    losses due to antiaircraft fire 21
    Midway plan 39–40
    numbers of aircraft 26
    order of battle at Midway 31–32
    planes lack of range 24
United States Marine Corps
    6th Marine Defense Battalion 15
    VMF-211 fighter squadron 43–44
    VMSB-241 squadron 47, 48, **82–84**, 88
United States Army Air Force (USAAF) 431st Bombardment Squadron 43

Vindicators dive-bomber, USN **82–84**, 88
Vireo, USN fleet tug 85

Waldron, Lt. Cdr. John 52
Wasp, USN carrier 22, 92
Wildcat fighters, USN 25, 26, **26**, 28, 43–44, 53, 69, 73, 89
    Coral Sea experience 28

Yamaguchi Tamon, Rear Adm. 13, 41, 49, 59, 60, 64, 73, 76
    bidding farewell 81
    second report of US carriers 77
Yamamoto Isoroku, Adm. 5, 7, 12, **12**, 13, 29, 39, 41, 48, 49, 85
    cancels Midway operation 81
    flawed planning and overconfidence 35–36, 37–38, 38–39
    Midway plans 8, 12
    new orders after USN strikes 60
    orders Akagi to be scuttled 59
    Pearl Harbor attack 12
    strategy to lure out and destroy the US Pacific Fleet 33–34, 35
Yanagimoto Ryusaku, Cpt. 13, 58
Yorktown, USN carrier 14, 15, **25**, **26**, 40, **45**, 46, 60, 91
    aftermath of IJN dive-bombing strike 63
    Air Group 25, 26
    attacked by IJN *I-168* 85
    combat air patrols (CAP) during *Hiryu* strikes 61, 62, **64–67**, 68–69, 72
    coordinating strikes 24
    Coral Sea 7, 18, 22, 43
    dead in the water **64**
    dive-bomber (VB-3) hits on *Soryu* **54–55**, 56
    escorts during *Hiryu* strike 61
    fire control 64
    Hiryu dive-bomber strike 61–63, **61**, 64, **66–67**, 72
    Hiryu torpedo-bomber strike 64–73, **65**, **68**, **69**, **70–72**
    at Pearl Harbor **23**
    reconnaissance 44, 73
    sinking 36, 85, **85**
    strike on *Haruna* **74–75**, 77
    torpedo-bomber (VT-3) strike on *Hiryu* 56–57, 58
    VF-3 fighters 65, 69
Yorktown class carriers, USN:
    antiaircraft defense 24
    armor protection 23

Zeros A6M fighters, IJN 19, **20**, 21, 25, 28, 44, 47, 49, 52
Zuiho, IJN light carrier **19**
Zuikaku, IJN carrier 23
    Coral Sea 7, 17